SPANISH SHORT STORIES

FOR BEGINNERS

25 Engaging Short Stories to Learn Spanish and Build
Your Vocabulary the Fun & Fast Way!

Table of Contents

Claim Your FREE Bonus!

LIMITED OFFER

We are giving away our **best-selling** Spanish Phrase Book to the first **200 customers!**

All you have to do is scan QR code with your phone camera below and follow the instructions to get your **FREE** free copy of:

"Easy Spanish Phrase Book: The 2000 Most Common Spanish Phrases For Travel and Everyday Life",

Valued at $15.99!

Hurry, once **200 readers** have clicked the link this offer will expire!

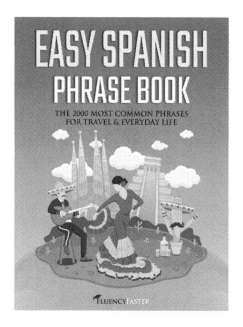

Introduction

So, you want to learn Spanish the quickest, easiest and most effect way possible?

Well you've made the right choice by buying this book.

Our mission is to cut your time to fluency in half, and this book is specifically designed to do just that.

Spanish Short Stories for Beginners was written to address an all too common problem which new Spanish learners encounter - the lack of simple, easy to understand reading material.

While most other "Learn Spanish books" focus on grammar, confusing tenses and other irrelevant material that leaves the student searching for words in the dictionary every 5 minutes, ours is different.

Not only is the "Death by Grammar" style of learning ineffective, it also wastes countless hours of time - not to mention BORING the hell out of the student!

We believe that learning Spanish should be fun and engaging.

It should challenge you, yes, but not to the extent that you want to give up before you even get started!

So how is this book different from the others?

Besides being fun, engaging and easy to read, each story is intelligently designed to tackle a specific set of basic vocabulary - words that you will use in everyday life.

Making sure to stimulate all of your senses - hearing, seeing, feeling, smelling and even tasting - we use highly descriptive language that makes Spanish words a breeze to remember.

This forces you to store everything in your long-term memory - remembering what you have learned for decades to come.

You will find that we use mostly present tense in the stories.

This helps you to focus on the dialogues, verbs, and nouns used - all while helping you to spot patterns in the Spanish language - which you can quickly start to apply.

With a wide variety of stories, we make sure to cover all the most important and commonly used vocabulary.

With stories like "The Million Dollar Race", "Magic at the Fair" and "A Brave Horse" you will be met by many intriguing characters who will take you on an effortless journey to Spanish mastery.

The characters in each story engage in interesting dialogue with one another, go through daily life situations, and use the most common, useful words and phrases.

The stories are simple, but not juvenile. They weren't written for children, but the language is still basic enough for beginners to easily follow the plot.

It's safe to say that this book is the closest you can come to "language immersion" without having to leave the country.

Right now, you are holding the key to bringing your Spanish studies to life.

How To Use This Book

All of the chapters in this book follow the same structure:

- A short story with several dialogs
- A summary of the story in Spanish
- A summary of the story in English
- A vocabulary list of important words/phrases with their English translation
- Questions to test your understanding of the story
- Answers to check if you were correct

Here are some recommendations for getting the most from the stories:

1) Start by reading the story all the way through. Don't get hung up on any particular words or phrases that you don't understand. Simply continue on and make a mental note of the word – there is no need to feel pressured to understanding everything you read from the first pass.

2) See how much of the plot you have understood without referring to a dictionary or another resource. It's completely normal not to understand everything in the story – simply jot down what you did understand in English.

3) Go onto reading the Spanish summary. See if it matches what you have understood from the plot.

4) Read the summary in English. See what you misunderstood and here the plot differs from what you first thought.

5) Move to the vocabulary list, have a look at the words you did not understand. Make sure you take note of them, and look them up in another sentence if you need more context.

6) Read the story through once more, but this time at a slower rate. Try to pick up the meaning of any words or phrases you didn't understand from the first pass. Use clues from the context of the words combine with what you remember reading in the summaries/vocabulary list.

7) Test yourself! Try answering the 5 comprehension questions that are at the end of each story. Write all of your answers down and then check them against the answer key provided.

8) Revisit the vocabulary list again. Are there still some words you didn't understand? If so...

9) Go through the story once more. This time pay close attention to the words and phrases you didn't understand. If you'd like, take the time to look them up in the vocabulary list as you move through the story.
Repeat from step one if needed.

10) Move on to the next chapter only when you feel like you are ready.

Chapter One

<u>Basic Vocabulary</u>

Mi Lugar Favorito - My Favorite Place

¡**H**ola, **mucho gusto**! Mi nombre es Firulais y les **voy a contar algo** emocionante. **Hoy** voy a **visitar** mi **lugar favorito**: ¡el parque! Tal vez, para algunos de ustedes ir al parque es algo **normal**, pero para mí es un lugar **fantástico**. Me encanta **ir** al parque, **porque allí** puedo **correr** libremente; recorro todo el parque a **gran velocidad. Este** parque es **muy grande**, con **bastantes** árboles; los **árboles** son **altos** y **muy verdes**. Otra **cosa** que **me gusta hacer** cuando **estoy** en el parque es **jugar** con la **pelota**. Me paso jugando con ella todo el **día** y ¡**me encanta!** Cada vez que **voy** al parque, hago muchos **amigos. Tengo** amigos muy **diferentes; algunos** son **altos**, otros **delgados, grandes, pequeños, bonitos o feos.** Les quiero mucho porque siempre juegan **conmigo.**

Otra cosa que me gusta hacer en el **parque** es **olfatear** el lugar. **Siempre** lo hago **cuando** voy para **allá**. Olfateo a los amigos que están **cerca**, a las **personas** que **caminan**, a los **niños**… el parque **tiene** muchos olores por **descubrir** y **hay** algunos muy **buenos**, como el olor de las **flores, el césped, el pino o la comida;** y otros **malos,** como la caca de los **animales.**

Yo vivo lejos del parque, **pero** esto **es** algo bueno porque así **puedo tomar** largos paseos **con** la persona a la que más quiero en el **mundo:** María. **Ella** me lleva por **calles** y **avenidas** de la **ciudad antes** de **llegar** al parque. **Normalmente veo** muchos **autos** cuando voy al parque con ella; algunos son de color **azul**, otros de color **rojo, amarillo, morado, blanco y negro.** Siempre **vamos** al parque a las **diez de la mañana** y no **regresamos** hasta las **tres de la tarde.**

María es **una** gran **mujer.** Siempre juega conmigo y me **cocina** comida **deliciosa.** Adoro **comer** bistec de **carne.** Me **compra** juguetes y siempre me saca a **pasear.** A veces **soy** algo **travieso** y le **muerdo** los **zapatos**, pero **me quiere** igualmente porque siempre voy a **ser su** guardián.

Pero no siempre fui tan **afortunado.** Cuando **era** pequeño, vivía en la calle, en **un** lugar muy **frío** y **peligroso** con mi **mamá.** Ella era muy **valiente** y siempre me protegía de **cualquier peligro.** Una **noche** yo tenía **hambre**, estaba **lloviendo** muy **fuerte** y mi mamá salió a **buscar comida. Tristemente,** no la volví a **ver nunca** más. Estuve **solo, triste,** con mucho frío y hambre durante mucho **tiempo**… aún la **extraño.** Por suerte, un día las **manos calientes** de María me **levantaron** del

suelo. Me llevó a su **casa**, donde me dio comida, **calor** y mucho **amor**. Fue el día más **feliz** de mi **vida** y nunca más estuve solo.

Hay muchos **perros** que no tienen la **misma suerte** que yo. Sería **genial** si más personas **rescataran a** más animales de la calle y les dieran un **hogar**. Salvarían una vida y, como **recompensa**, tendrían amor **puro para siempre. Fue** un **placer hablar** con **ustedes**, ¡**Adiós**! ¡Guau, guau!

Resumen de la historia

Firulais es un perro alegre y juguetón. Nos cuenta lo mucho que le gusta ir al parque y cómo le encanta correr, olfatear, conocer nuevos amigos y jugar. También nos relata su triste historia; Firulais era un cachorro abandonado que vivía en la calle con su madre hasta que una noche esta murió buscando comida. Afortunadamente, María, su futura dueña, lo rescató y le dio mucho amor. Ahora viven juntos muy felices.

Summary of the story

Firulais is a happy and playful dog. He tells us how much he loves going to the park and how he loves to run, sniff, meet new friends and play. He also tells us his sad story of being an abandoned puppy who lived in the street with his mother after she died one night looking for food. Fortunately, he was rescued by Maria, his future owner, who would give him lots of love and live happily together.

<u>Vocabulary List</u>

Some Spanish words have several meanings. Try to relate them using the context of the story.

- **Adiós**: Goodbye.
- **Afortunado**: Lucky.
- **Ahí**: There.
- **Algo**: Something.
- **Algunos**: Some.
- **Allá**: There/Over there.
- **Alto**: Tall.
- **Amarillo**: Yellow.
- **Peligro**: Danger.
- **Amigo**: Friend.
- **Amor**: Love.
- **Animales**: Animals. (Plural)
- **Antes**: Before.
- **Árboles**: Trees. (Plural)
- **Auto**: Car.
- **Avenida**: Avenue.
- **Azul**: Blue.
- **Bastantes**: Quite a lot.
- **Blanco**: White.
- **Bonito**: Pretty/Nice.
- **Bueno**: Good.
- **Buscar**: Search/Look.
- **Calientes**: Hot.
- **Calle**: Street.

- **Calor**: Heat.
- **Caminar**: Walk.
- **Carne**: Meat.
- **Casa**: House.
- **Cerca**: Near/Close to.
- **Césped**: Grass.
- **Ciudad**: City.
- **Cocinar**: Cooking.
- **Comer**: Eat.
- **Comida**: Food.
- **Comprar**: Buy.
- **Con**: With.
- **Conmigo**: With me.
- **Contaré**: I will tell
- **Correr**: Run.
- **Cosa**: Thing.
- **Cualquier**: Any.
- **Cuando**: When.
- **Delgado**: Thin.
- **Delicioso(a)**: Delicious.
- **Descubrir**: Discover, find.
- **Día**: Day.
- **Diez de la mañana:** Ten o'clock in the morning.
- **El**: The (Do not confuse with "él").
- **Él**: He.
- **Ella**: She.
- **Emocionante**: Amazing/Exciting.
- **Era**: Was.
- **Es**: Is.
- **Este**: This
- **Estoy**: I am.
- **Extrañar**: Miss.
- **Fantástico**: Fantastic.
- **Favorito**: Favorite.
- **Feliz**: Happy.
- **Feo**: Ugly.
- **Flores**: Flowers. (Plural)
- **Frío**: Cold.
- **Fue**: Was.
- **Fuerte**: Strong/hard.
- **Genial**: Great/Awesome.
- **Gran**: Great/Big.
- **Grande**: Big.
- **Guau**: Woof

- **Hablar**: Talk/Speak.
- **Hacer**: Do/make.
- **Hambre**: Hungry.
- **Hasta**: Until.
- **Hay**: There is/There are.
- **Hogar**: Home.
- **Hoy**: Today.
- **Ir**: Go to.
- **Jugar**: Play.
- **Largo**: Large/Tall/Long.
- **Lejos**: Far/Away.
- **Levantar**: Lift/Rise.
- **Llegar**: Arrive.
- **Lloviendo**: Raining.
- **Lugar**: Place.
- **Malo**: Bad.
- **Mamá**: Mother.
- **Manos**: Hands. (Plural)
- **Más**: More
- **Me encanta**: I love it.
- **Me gusta**: I like it.
- **Mismo(a)**: Same.
- **Morado**: Purple.
- **Morder**: Bite.
- **Mucho**: A lot.
- **Mucho gusto**: Nice to meet you.
- **Mujer**: Woman.
- **Mundo**: World.
- **Muy**: Very.
- **Muy grande**: Very big.
- **Negro**: Black.
- **Niños**: Kids.
- **Noche**: Night.
- **Normal**: Normal.
- **Normalmente**: Normally.
- **Nunca**: Never.
- **Olfatear**: Smell/Sniff.
- **Otra vez**: Again.
- **Otro**: Other.
- **Parque**: Park.
- **Pasear**: Walk.
- **Peligroso**: Dangerous.
- **Pelota**: Ball.
- **Pequeño**: Little.
- **Pero**: But.

- **Perro**: Dog.
- **Persona**: Person.
- **Pino**: Pine.
- **Placer**: Pleasure.
- **Por**: For/By
- **Para siempre**: For ever.
- **Porque**: Because.
- **Puedo**: I can.
- **Puro**: Pure.
- **Querer/Quiero**: I love/I like/I Want.
- **Recompensa**: Reward.
- **Regresar**: Return/Come back.
- **Rescatar**: Rescue.
- **Rojo**: Red.
- **Ser**: be.
- **Siempre**: Always.
- **Solo**: Alone/Only.
- **Soy**: I am.
- **Su**: Her/His/Their.
- **Suelo**: Ground/Floor.
- **Suerte**: Lucky.
- **Tengo**: I have.
- **Tiempo**: Time.
- **Tiene**: Has.
- **Tomar**: Take.
- **Travieso**: Naughty/Playful
- **Tres de la tarde**: Three o'clock in the afternoon.
- **Triste**: Sad.
- **Tristemente**: Sadly.
- **Un(a)**: a, an.
- **Ustedes**: You.
- **Valiente**: Brave.
- **Vamos**: Go to/Let's go.
- **Velocidad**: Speed.
- **Veo**: I See/I watch/I look.
- **Ver**: See/look.
- **Verde**: Green.
- **Vida**: Life.
- **Visitar**: Visit
- **Vivo**: I live.
- **Voy**: I am going.
- **Yo**: I.
- **Zapatos**: Shoes.

Questions about the story

1. ¿Cuál es el nombre del narrador de la historia?

    a. María.
    b. Firulais.
    c. La madre de Firulais.
    d. Ninguna de las anteriores.

2. ¿Cuál es la comida que le cocina María a Firulais?

    a. Arroz.
    b. Pollo.
    c. Bistec de carne.
    d. Hot dogs.

3. ¿En dónde vivía Firulais antes que lo rescatara María?

    a. En la calle.
    b. En un Castillo.
    c. En un Parque.

4. ¿Qué le sucedió a la madre de Firulais en la historia?

    a. Se murió.
    b. Se mudó.
    c. Se quedó con Firulais.
    d. Lo vendió.

5. ¿Qué es Firulais?

    a. Gato.
    b. Niño.
    c. Perro.
    d. Un hombre.

Answers

1. B - Who is the narrator of the story?
2. C - What food does Maria cook for Firulais?
3. A - Where did Firulais live before Mary rescued him?
4. A - What happened to Firulais' mother in the story?
5. C - What is Firulais?

Chapter Two

Basic Vocabulary (Accion, movement)

Un sueño hecho realidad/A Dream Come True

Héctor era un **joven** con un gran **sueño**, ¡**ser jugador** de **Baloncesto**!y ser el **mejor**. Su **hermano mayor** es su mayor **inspiración**. Su hermano Hugo es **cinco años mayor, alto, moreno,** de **brazos** y **piernas largas** que le **permiten tirar desde** lejos y **correr rápido**. Héctor **también quería** ser un jugador **profesional**.

Cerca de su casa **había** una **cancha**, para **llegar, ellos** solían **subir** dos **calles,** y **cruzar** a la **izquierda otras cuatro**. Él **acompañaba** todos los días a Hugo a esta cancha, le gustaba **verlo** jugar **Cada** uno de sus **partidos**. Él se **emocionaba** cuando Hugo **jugaba** con **pasión** y **entrega**, eso **logró** que Héctor **amara** mucho el .Baloncesto. Pero **tristemente** una **lesión** muy fuerte hizo que Hugo **abandonara** su **meta** de ser jugador de balocensto profesional. Un día en un juego, un jugador del equipo **contrario** hizo una **falta** a **propósito** y **lamentablemente** lo lesiono.

Fue un día muy triste para él, para Héctor y para su **familia**. Inspirándose en su hermano, Héctor se **propuso** a **entrenar** y **trabajar duro** para **cumplir** su sueño, **correr, saltar, tortar** y **rebotar** pelotas **todo el día**. Un día llego al **barrio** donde vivía Héctor un **entrenador** de un **equipo** profesional, queriendo **reclutar** jugadores jóvenes de **bajos recursos** y **darles** una **oportunidad**. Los **aspirantes** tuvieron **varias pruebas**, algunas de estas fueron: correr **rápidamente** contra **reloj, saltar arriba y abajo tantas veces** como sea **posible, tiros de corta, media y larga distancia**; driblear a gran **velocidad** en **distintas direcciones**, a la **derecha**, a la izquierda, en **diagonal**, para **adelante** y para **atrás**.

Al **principio** Héctor estaba muy **nervioso** y tímido, pero al ver a su hermano y su familia en las **gradas apoyándolo**., Héctor **ganó confianza**, y comenzó a jugar muy **bien**, incluso mejor que sus **rivales**. Al fin llego la **última** prueba, **que** consistía en Jugar un partido **completo**, cinco **contra** cinco. Al **terminar** el partido Héctor fue el jugador más **valioso**, hizo **cuarenta puntos** y tuvo un **promedio de quince rebotes**. El entrenador se acercó a él, y le dijo que estaba en el equipo. Toda su familia se sintió muy **orgullosa; en especial** su hermano. **Finalmente,** Héctor hizo **realidad** su sueño.

Resumen de la historia

Héctor es un joven humilde y su mayor sueño es ser un gran jugador de baloncesto. La persona que le inspira mayor admiración es su hermano Hugo, al que siempre acompañaba a los partidos. Debido a circunstancias inesperadas, Hugo no puede jugar más, pero esto le da a Héctor un motivo para trabajar duro y hacer realidad su mayor sueño. Un día, una oportunidad llama a su puerta y consigue hacer realidad su más grande deseo.

Summary of the story

Hector is a humble young man whose biggest dream is to be a great basketball player. His greatest admiration was his older brother Hugo, whom he always accompanied to all his games. Due to unexpected circumstances, Hugo could no longer play, but this gives Hector a reason to work hard and make his biggest dream come true. One day an opportunity knocks on his door, and he manages to make his greatest dream come true.

Vocabulary List

- **A propósito:** On purpose.
- **A veces:** Sometimes.
- **Abajo:** Down/Below.
- **Abandonar:** Quit/Abandon/Drop.
- **Acompañar:** Go with/Accompany.
- **Adelante:** Forward/Ahead.
- **Alto:** Tall/Large.
- **Amará:** will love.
- **Años:** Year.
- **Apoyando:** Supporting/. Encouraging
- **Arriba:** Up/Above.
- **Aspirantes:** Candidates/Applicants. (Plural)
- **Atrás:** Behind/Back.
- **Bajos recursos:** Poor.
- **Baloncesto:** Basketball.
- **Barrio:** Neighborhood.
- **Bien:** Good/Fine.
- **Cada:** Each/Every.
- **Calles:** Streets. (Plural)
- **Cancha:** Court/Field.
- **Cerca:** Close/Near.
- **Cinco:** Five.
- **Completo:** Complete.
- **Confianza:** Trust/Confidence.
- **Contra:** Against/Versus.
- **Contrario:** Opposite.
- **Correr:** Run.
- **Corriendo:** Running.
- **Corta:** Short/Brief.
- **Cruza:** Cross
- **Cuarenta:** Forty.
- **Cuatro:** Four.
- **Cumplir:** Achieve/Fulfil.
- **Darles:** Give them.
- **Derecha:** Right.

- **Desde:** Since.
- **Diagonal:** Diagonal.
- **Direcciones:** Directions.
- **Distancia:** Distance.
- **Duro:** Hard.
- **Él.** He.
- **Ellos:** They.
- **Emocionaba:** Excited.
- **En Especial:** Specially.
- **Entrega:** Dedication/Delivery.
- **Entrenador:** Coach/Trainer.
- **Entrenar:** Train.
- **Equipo:** Team.
- **Falta:** Foul.
- **Familia:** Family.
- **Finalmente:** Finally.
- **Fuertemente:** Strongly.
- **Ganó:** Won.
- **Gradas:** Stands. (Plural)
- **Había:** There was.
- **Hermano:** Brother.
- **Inspiración:** Inspiration.
- **Intimidado:** Intimidated.
- **Izquierda:** Left.
- **Joven:** Young.
- **Jugaba:** Played.
- **Jugador:** Player.
- **La cual consiste:** Which consists of.
- **Lamentablemente:** Unfortunately.
- **Larga:** Large/Long.
- **Lejos:** Far/Away.
- **Lesión:** Injury.
- **Llegar:** Arrive.
- **Logró:** Succeeded.
- **Mayor:** Older.
- **Media:** Middle.
- **Mejor:** Better/Best.

- **Meta:** Goal/Dream.
- **Moreno:** Dark-skinned.
- **Nervioso:** Nervous.
- **Oportunidad:** Opportunity/Chance.
- **Orgullosa:** Proud.
- **Partidos:** Games/Matches. (Plural)
- **Pasión:** Passion.
- **Permiten:** Allow.
- **Piernas:** Legs.
- **Posible:** Possible.
- **Principio:** Beginning/Start.
- **Profesional:** Professional.
- **Promedio:** Average.
- **Propuso:** Proposed/Suggested.
- **Pruebas:** Tests. (Plural)
- **Puntos:** Points. (Plural)
- **Quería:** I love/I want.
- **Quince:** Fifteen.
- **Rápido:** Fast/Quick.
- **Rápidamente:** Quickly.
- **Realidad:** Come true/Reality/Fact/Truth.
- **Rebotando:** Bouncing.
- **Rebotes:** Bounces.
- **Reclutar:** Recruit.
- **Reloj:** Clock/Timer.
- **Rivales:** Rivals. (Plural)
- **Saltando:** Jumping.
- **Saltar:** Jump.
- **Ser:** Be.
- **Subir:** Go up/Climb/Rise/Turn up.
- **Sueño:** Dream/Goal
- **También:** Also/ As well.
- **Tantas:** So many.
- **Terminar:** Finish.
- **Tirar:** Shot/Throw.
- **Tiros:** Shots. (Plural)
- **Todo el día:** All day.
- **Trabajar:** Work.
- **Tristemente:** Sadly.

- **Trotar:** Jog.
- **Última:** Last/Latest/Ultimate
- **Valioso:** Valuable.
- **Varias:** Several.
- **Velocidad:** Speed.
- **Vencer:** Beat/Defeat.

Questions about the story

1. ¿De dónde sacó Héctor su inspiración?

    a. De un jugador.
    b. De su padre.
    c. De su hermano.
    d. De un equipo.

2. ¿Cuántos puntos anotó Héctor en el partido final?

    a. 20 puntos.
    b. 40 puntos.
    c. 15 puntos.
    d. 30 puntos.

3. ¿Cuál fue la causa de la lesión de Hugo?

    a. Se cayó.
    b. Tuvo un accidente.
    c. Lo lesiono otro jugador.
    d. Ninguna de las anteriores.

4. ¿Cómo entró Héctor en el equipo?

    a. Por la universidad.
    b. Por un concurso.
    c. Por un amigo.
    d. Ninguna de las anteriores.

5. ¿Cuál era el mayor sueño de Héctor?

    a. Jugar baloncesto.
    b. Jugar beisbol.
    c. Jugar Futbol
    d. Ser abogado.

Answers

1. **C** - Where did Hector get his inspiration?
2. **B** - How many points did Hector score in the final game?
3. **C** - What was the cause of Hugo's injury?
4. **D** - How did Hector join the team?
5. **A** - What was Hector's biggest dream?

Chapter Three

Magia en la feria/Magic at the Fair

Diana es una **niña** muy **dulce** de **seis años**, su **cabello** es **ondulado** de color **rubio claro**, que le llega hasta sus **hombros**. Su mayor **deseo** era ir a la **feria** porque siempre pasan por ahí cuando sus **padres** la llevaban a la **escuela**. También pasaban muchos **comerciales** de la feria **mientras** ella veía **televisión**, porque ella es muy fan de las **caricaturas**. Llego, el día de su **cumpleaños** sus padres, Carlos y Andrea **decidieron regalarle** un **viaje** a la feria. La niña **saltaba** de emoción y **felicidad**. Sus padres la **vistieron** para este gran día, Diana vestía unos pequeños **zapatos** negros, un **vestido rosado**, una **camiseta blanca** y un pequeño **suéter amarillo**. Diana era una niña muy **curiosa**, quería saber el **porqué** de todo, ¿**Por qué** el **sol** era tan **brillante** y **cálido**? ¿Por qué el **pasto** era verde y **suave**? ¿Por qué el **cielo** es azul? ¿Por qué la **luna sale** de **noche**? Y así con todo.

El **viaje** en **auto** fue muy **alegre**, su padre **escuchaba música** en la radio mientras **manejaba**, su madre **se terminaba** de **maquillar**, y ella **observaba** todo con **emoción** desde la **ventana**. **Poco a poco** se van acercando más al **divertido lugar**, Diana está **impaciente**, ella quiere llegar lo **antes posible**, y **montarse** en todas las **atracciones mecánicas, comer algodón de azúcar, manzanas acarameladas, palomitas de maíz, caramelos**, chocolates, etc. **Finalmente**, llegaron y quedó **encantada** por las **luces brillantes**, los colores **resplandecientes**, y los **sonidos** de las personas **riendo** y **pasándola bien**.

Diana se quería **subir** en todos los **juegos mecánicos**, los que más le **gustaron** fueron **aquellos** que la hacían **girar rápidamente**. Ella estaba muy **agradecida** con sus padres porque se estaba **divirtiendo como nunca**. Toda la familia **disfrutó** y se divirtió en aquella feria, Carlos con Diana jugaron y **ganaron varios premios**, como **peluches, muñecas** y otros **recuerdos**. Todo iba bien, cuando **de repente** a Diana le dieron ganas de ir al **baño**, y le **pidió** a su padre que la acompañara, mientras **miraba** todo a su **alrededor** le llamo la **atención** un **maravilloso payaso** que estaba **haciendo reír** y divertir a todos. Su nombre era Popi, un payaso de grandes zapatos **azules**, una **nariz roja** muy grande y brillante; cabello **desordenado** verde, **ojos** grandes **pintados** de **amarillo** y **naranja vibrante**.

Diana estaba emocionada con ese **personaje** tan **único, jamás** había visto algo **parecido**. Ese fue un gran día, **conoció** un lugar maravilloso y lleno de **magia**.

Resumen de la historia

Diana es una niña muy dulce y curiosa, su mayor deseo era ir a la feria, sus padres sabían esto, y como regalo de cumpleaños la llevaron a la feria. La pequeña estaba muy contenta. Al llegar la pequeña quedó deslumbrada por todos los colores, olores y sonidos, los cuales se abrían paso ante ella. En este sitio conoce un personaje muy particular quien divierte y hace reír a todos, un maravilloso payaso que se roba su atención.

Summary of the story

Diana is a sweet and curious little girl, her greatest wish was to go to the fair, her parents knew this, and as a birthday present, they took her to the fair. The little girl was delighted. Upon arrival, the little girl was dazzled by all the colors, smells and sounds, which opened before her. In this place, she met a very particular character who amused and made everyone laugh, a wonderful clown who stole her attention.

Vocabulary List

- **Acercando:** Approaching.
- **Agradecida:** grateful.
- **Alegre:** Joyful.
- **Algodón de azúcar:** Cotton candy.
- **Alrededor:** Around.
- **Amarillo:** Yellow.
- **Antes:** Before/Once.
- **Años:** Years/Years old. (Plural)
- **Aquellos:** Those.
- **Atención:** Attention.
- **Atracciones mecánicas:** Mechanical rides
- **Auto:** Car.
- **Baño:** Bathroom.
- **Blanca:** White.
- **Brillante:** Brilliant/Shiny.
- **Cabello:** Hair.
- **Cálido:** Warm.
- **Camiseta: T-shirt.**
- **Caramelos:** Candies. (Plural)
- **Caricaturas:** Cartoons. (Plural)
- **Cielo:** Sky.
- **Claro:** Clear/Light/Of course.
- **Comer:** Eat.
- **Comerciales:** Commercials. (Plural)
- **Como:** Like/As.
- **Conoció :**Meet/Knew.
- **Cumpleaños:** Birthday.
- **Curiosa:** Curious.
- **De repente:** Suddenly.
- **Decidieron:** They decided.
- **Deseo:** Wish/Desire.
- **Desordenado:** Messy.
- **Disfrutó:** Enjoyed.
- **Divertido:** Fun/Enjoyable.
- **Divirtiendo:** Having fun.
- **Dulce:** Sweet.
- **Emoción:** Excitement.
- **Encantada:** Delighted.
- **Escuchaba:** Listened.
- **Escuela:** School.
- **Felicidad:** Happiness.
- **Feria:** Fair.
- **Finalmente:** Finally.
- **Ganaron:** Won.
- **Girar:** Spin/Turn.
- **Gustaron:** Liked.
- **Haciendo:** Making/Doing.
- **Hombros:** Shoulders. (Plural)
- **Impaciente:** Impatient.
- **Jamás:** Never.
- **Llamar:** Call.
- **Luces:** Lights.
- **Lugar:** Places.
- **Luna:** Moon.
- **Magia:** Magic.
- **Manejaba:** Drive.
- **Manzanas acarameladas:** Caramel apples.
- **Maquillar:** Make up.
- **Maravilloso:** Wonderful.
- **Mientras:** While.
- **Miraba:** Look.
- **Montarse:** Get on.
- **Muñecas:** Dolls. (Plural)
- **Música:** Music.
- **Naranja:** Orange.
- **Nariz:** Nose.
- **Niña:** Girl.
- **Noche:** Night.
- **Nunca:** Never.
- **Observaba:** Watch.
- **Ojos:** Eyes. (Plural)
- **Ondulado:** Wavy.
- **Padres:** Parents.
- **Palomitas de maíz:** Pop corn.

- **Parecido:** Similar.
- **Pasándola bien:** Having a good time.
- **Pasto:** Grass.
- **Payaso:** Clown.
- **Peluches:** Teddy Bears.
- **Personaje:** Character.
- **Pidió:** Asked.
- **Pintados:** Painted.
- **Poco a poco:** Little by little.
- **Por qué:** Why.
- **Porqué:** Reason/Cause.
- **Posible:** Possible.
- **Premios:** Rewards/Prizes. (Plural)
- **Rápidamente:** Quickly.
- **Recuerdos:** Souvenirs/Memories.
- **Regalarle:** Gift to.
- **Reír:** Laugh.
- **Resplandecientes:** Resplendent/Radiant.
- **Riendo:** Laughing.
- **Roja:** Red.
- **Rosado:** Pink.
- **Rubio:** Blonde.
- **Sale:** Comes out.
- **Saltar:** Jumping.
- **Se terminaba:** It ended.
- **Seis:** Six.
- **Sol:** Sun.
- **Sonidos:** Sounds. (Plural)
- **Suave:** Soft.
- **Subir:** Get on.
- **Suéter:** Sweater.
- **Televisión:** TV.
- **Único:** Unique/Only.
- **Varios:** Several/Some.
- **Ventana:** Window.
- **Vestido:** Dress.
- **Viaje:** Journey.
- **Vibrantes:** Vibrant.
- **Vistieron:** Wear/Dressed.
- **Zapatos:** Shoes.

Questions about the story

1. ¿Por qué los padres llevaron a la niña a la feria?

    a. Porque se portó bien.
    b. Porque sacóbuenas calificaciones.
    c. Porque era su cumpleaños.
    d. Porque perdieron una apuesta.

2. ¿Cuántos años tiene Diana?

    a. Cuatro.
    b. Seis.
    c. Ocho.
    d. Diez.

3. ¿ Quién era el personaje que le llamó la atención de la niña?

    a. Bombero.
    b. Policía.
    c. Mago.
    d. Payaso.

4. ¿ De qué color es el cabello de Diana?

    a. Negro.
    b. Rojo.
    c. Castaño.
    d. Ninguna de las anteriores

5. ¿Qué premios ganaron en la feria?

    a. Peluches y Muñecas.
    b. Dulces.
    c. Autos de juguete.
    d. Ropa.

Answers

1. C - Why did the parents take the girl to the fair?
2. B - How old is Diana?
3. D - What was the character that caught the girl's attention?
4. D - What color is Diana's hair?
5. A - What prizes did they win at the fair?

Chapter Four

Basic Verbs.

Amor y nervios/Love and Nerves

Hola yo **soy** Pablo. Hoy te voy a **contar** la historia de mi primera cita. Sofía es una chica muy inteligente y brillante, la **veo** todos los días en la universidad, pero **atreverme hablarle** era algo muy difícil para mí. Un día mi mejor amigo Juan me **impulsó** a **tener** la iniciativa.

"Pablo, siempre **miras** a Sofía durante los descansos, pero no te atreves a hablarle, tienes que tener el valor y **acercarte** a ella, de lo contrario nunca la vas a **conocer**", dice Juan.

"No es tan fácil, me **da** miedo que ella me **rechace** y no me **quiera** hablar", dice Pablo con nerviosismo.

"Debes **arriesgarte**, y así **vas** a **saber**, si ella te quiere hablar o no", **responde** Juan, dándole ánimos y valor a su amigo.

Luego de mucho **pensar** al final lo **hice**. Ella **estaba sentada** en unas bancas **leyendo** un libro, **camine** hacia ella y **comenzamos** a hablar.

"Hola Sofía, ¿cómo estás?", pregunta pablo, "¿Me puedo **sentar** aquí contigo?".

"Hola, ¡muy bien! Y ¿tú, cómo está?", responde Sofía sorprendida "¡Si claro siéntate!".

"Yo **estoy** genial, **estaba** por aquí, y **decidí** sentarme a **charlar** contigo", dice Pablo algo nervio.

Ella era realmente divertida y muy amable, le **pregunté** sobre sus gustos, ya que me encanta **escucharla** hablar. Una de las cosas que **menciono** era que **adoraba** el cine y **comer** palomitas de maíz. Cuando **finalizó** nuestra charla, le pedí **intercambiar** números.

"¿Me **darías** tu número para **seguir** en contacto?", pregunta Pablo.

"¡Claro que sí! ¡Me encantaría!, ¿tienes lápiz y papel para **anotarlo**?", responde Sofía sorprendida.

Y así **quedamos**. Unos días después le **escribí** si quería **ir** al cine conmigo, ella aceptó y **arreglamos** el día y la hora. Camino al cine **iba** muy nervioso. Al llegar **fuimos** directo a **comprar** las entradas.

"¿Qué tipo de película te gustaría **ver**?", pregunta Pablo.

"Esa de comedia se ve divertida e interesante", responde Sofía.

"Veamos esa", dice Pablo.

Luego de comprar las entradas, fuimos por palomitas, chocolates y gaseosas. Yo estaba tan nervioso que **derrame** mi gaseosa. Sofía **empezó** a **reír**, pero luego me **dijo** que no me **preocupase**. Compramos otra gaseosa, y **entramos** a la sala de cine para ver la película. Ella comenzó a **comer** palomitas, yo también comía, **acompañándolas** con chocolate. Ella se **sorprendió** por **verme combinar** esos sabores entre salado y dulce. Pero luego la **convencí** de **probarlos** y le encantó.

Al **terminar** la película, me ofrecí a **llevarla a su** casa. Ella **aceptó**, y nos **dirigimos** al carro, **vivía** en un edificio muy bonito. Al **bajar** del carro, me **dijo** que se **había** divertido mucho, y le **gustaría** volver a **salir** conmigo. Me **fui** a mi casa muy feliz, y así termina mi historia de como fue mi primera cita con la chica que tiempo después **sería** mi prometida, si así es, le **propuse** matrimonio y ella aceptó.

Ya **saben**, si realmente les **gusta** alguien no duden en **arriesgarse** a **dar** el primer paso, pueden terminar **conociendo** a la persona que **podrá** ser la más maravillosa de su vida.

Resumen de la historia

Pablo nos cuenta la historia de cómo fue su primera cita con su prometida, como verla todos los días en la universidad, hizo que se enamorara de ella, y como su mejor amigo lo impulsó a tener el valor para hablarle a la chica de sus sueños. Después de una tarde maravillosa en el cine, al final todo sale muy bien para Pablo, y tiene una linda cita con Sofía.

Summary of the story

Pablo tells us the story of his first date with his fiancée, how seeing her every day in college made him fall in love with her, and how his best friend pushed him to have the courage to talk to the girl of his dreams. After a delightful evening at the movies, in the end, everything turns out very well for Pablo, and he has a nice date with Sofia.

Vocabulary list

The translations and the verbs between the parenthesis are in their infinitive grammatical form. Some Spanish verbs have several meanings. Try to relate them using the context of the story.

- **Aceptó (Aceptar):** Accept.
- **Acercarte (Acercar):** Approach/Bring.
- **Acompañándolas (Acompañar):** Accompany/Go with.
- **Adoraba (Adorar):** Adore/Worship/Love.
- **Anotarlo (Anotar):** Mark/Write.
- **Arreglamos (Arreglar):** Fix/Repair.
- **Arriesgarse (Arriesgar):** Risk/Take a risk/Endanger.
- **Arriesgarte (Arriesgar):** Risk/Take a risk/Endanger.
- **Atreverme (Atreverse):** Dare.
- **Bajar:** Lower/Get out/Decrease/Go down.
- **Camine (Caminar):** Walk.
- **Charlar:** Chat.
- **Combinar:** Combine/Mix/Blend.
- **Comenzamos (Comenzar):** Start/Begin.
- **Comer:** Eat.
- **Comprar:** Buy.
- **Conocer:** Know.
- **Conociendo (Conocer):** Know.
- **Contar:** Tell.
- **Convencí (Convencer):** Convince/Persuade.
- **Da (Dar):** Give/Deliver.
- **Darías (Dar):** Give/Deliver.
- **Decidí (Decidir)** Give/Deliver.
- **Derrame (Derramar)** Pour/Spill.
- **Dijo (Decir):** Say.
- **Dijo (Decir):** Say.
- **Dirigimos (Dirigir):** Direct/Manage.
- **Empezó (Empezar):** Start/Begin/Take off.
- **Entramos (Entrar):** Enter.
- **Escribí (Escribir):** Write.
- **Escucharla (Escuchar):** Listen.
- **Estaba (Estar):** Be.
- **Estoy (Estar):** Be.
- **Finalizó (Finalizar):** Finish/End.
- **Fui (Ir):** Go.
- **Fuimos (ir):** Go.
- **Gusta (Gustar):** Like.
- **Gustaría (Gustar):** Like.
- **Había (Hay):** There is/There are.
- **Hablarle (Hablar):** Speak/Talk.
- **Hice (Hacer):** Make/Do.

- **Iba (Ir):** Go.
- **Impulsó (Impulsar):** Push/Propel/Boost.
- **Intercambiar:** Exchange.
- **Ir:** Go.
- **Leyendo (Leer):**Real.
- **Llevarla (Llevar):** Carry/Give a ride.
- **Miras (Mirar):**Look.
- **Pensar:** Think.
- **Podrá (Poder):** Able/Can/May.
- **Pregunté (Preguntar):** Ask.
- **Preocupase (Preocupar):** Worry.
- **Probarlos (Probar):** Try.
- **Propuse (Proponer):** Propose/Suggest.
- **Quedamos (Quedar):** Meet/Remain.
- **Quiera (Querer):** Want/Like/Desire.
- **Rechace (Rechazar):** Reject.
- **Reír:** Laugh.
- **Responde (Responder):** Reply/Respond/Answer.
- **Saben (Saber):** Know.
- **Salir:** Exit/Leave.
- **Seguir:** Keep/Follow/Continue.
- **Sentada (Sentarse):** Sit.
- **Sería (Ser):** Be.
- **Sorprendió (Sorprender):**
- **Soy (Ser):** Be.
- **Tener:** Have/Had.
- **Terminar:** Complete/Finish/End.
- **Vas (Ir):** Go.
- **Veo (Ver):** Watch/See/Look.
- **Verme (Ver):** Watch/See/Look.
- **Vivía (Vivir):** Live.

Questions about the story

1. ¿Cuál es el mayor gusto de Sofía?

    a. Ir a la universidad.
    b. Ir al cine.
    c. Escuchar música.
    d. Hablar con pablo.

2. ¿Por qué Pablo no le hablaba a Sofía?

    a. Miedo al rechazo.
    b. Porque tenía novio.
    c. Porque olía feo.
    d. Ninguna de las anteriores.

3. ¿De qué género era la película que verían en el cine?

    a .Horror.
    b. Romántica.
    c. Drama.
    d. Ninguna de las anteriores.

4. ¿Qué comió Pablo en el cine?

    a. Palomitas de Maíz con Chocolate.
    b. Chocolate y algodón de azúcar.
    c. Hot dogs.
    d. Palomitas de Maíz.

5. ¿Qué son Pablo y Sofía en el futuro?

    a. Casados.
    b. Divorciados.
    c. Comprometidos.
    d. Novios.

Answers

1. B - What is Sofia's favorite thing?
2. A - Why didn't Pablo talk to Sofia?
3. D - What genre was the movie they would see in the theater?
4. A - What did Pablo eat at the movies?
5. C - What are Pablo and Sofia in the future?

Chapter Five

Una carrera de un millón de dólares | A Million Dollar Race

Aficionados de la velocidad, el **riesgo** y la **adrenalina**. ¡Bienvenidos!. **Hoy** nos **espera** una **carrera** muy emocionante. Esta **pista** es una de las mejores, con muchas **curvas**, muy **cerradas**, largas **rectas**, esta pista se **encuentra rodeada** de **bellas montañas**, y **árboles** frondosos. Hoy hay un **clima perfecto**, hay un **cielo despejado** y azul; con **viento**, mucho **sol** y **calor**, sin **nubes cerca**, y sin pronósticos de **lluvia**.

En **primer lugar** tenemos al **vehículo número trece** del **piloto mexicano** Pedro Sánchez, de **segundo** lugar el vehículo con el número **diecisiete** del piloto **argentino** Andrés Rodríguez, en el **tercer** lugar está el piloto **colombiano** con el número **ocho**, en el **cuarto** lugar el piloto **venezolano** Cristian Guerra con el número **veintidós**, en el **quinto** lugar el **chileno** José Guzmán con el número **treinta y nueve**, en el **sexto** lugar el piloto **brasilero** Alex Cavalera con el número **cuarenta y uno**, con el **séptimo** lugar el **peruano** Robert Pizarro con el número **sesenta y tres**, en el **octavo** puesto el piloto **español** Rubén Castillo con el número **cincuenta y cinco**, de **noveno** lugar el piloto **estadounidense** Carl Maxwell con el número **ochenta** y en el **décimo** lugar el piloto **inglés** Wayne Bate con el **cien**.

Comienza la carrera tomando el **liderato** el número cuarenta y uno, detrás le sigue el piloto con el número veintidós. Esto **promete** una buena carrera, el piloto Pedro Sánchez **toma** la curva hacia la **derecha** a gran velocidad **intentando pasar** al piloto al Andrés Rodríguez. El auto número ocho **al parecer** va muy **lento** y es **posible** que tenga que **cambiar** una **llanta**.

El piloto estadounidense y el inglés **batallan** en la recta **acelerando** a la **máxima capacidad** de sus vehículos. El vehículo número treinta y nueve **frena repentinamente**, **mientras** el auto número sesenta y tres lo **rebasa**. El auto número ocho quedo **detrás** de todos los vehículos, mientras que el piloto brasileño se encuentra **adelante** como líder. El piloto número cuarenta y cinco, **lamentablemente abandono** la carrera porque se **salió** del **camino** y choco con la **barrera** de **protección**. El **accidente** no **fue grave** y se **encuentra** bien.

Están en la recta final, y vienen los vehículos a gran velocidad. Se agita la bandera a cuadros y el ganador de la carrera fue el piloto brasileño Alex Cavalera, de segundo el venezolano Cristian Guerra, y en el tercer lugar el piloto mexicano Pedro Sánchez.

Esta ha sido una carrera **fantástica** llena de **emociones**. Llego la **hora** de entregar los **premios** y los **trofeos**. El primer premio es de **un millón** de dólares, el segundo premio es de **cien mil** dólares y el tercer premio es de **cincuenta mil** dólares. **Gracias** por acompañarnos a esta **transmisión** los esperamos en la **próxima** carrera.

Resumen de la historia

Nos espera una gran carrera, donde sabremos las acciones y maniobras de un grupo de pilotos, amantes de la velocidad y la adrenalina. En una carrera para lograr el tan ansiado primer premio, nada más y nada menos que de un millón de dólares. Los pilotos de diferentes nacionalidades dejarán todo para ser el campeón.

Summary of the story

A great race awaits us, where we will know the actions and maneuvers of a group of drivers, lovers of speed and adrenaline in a race to achieve the so desired first prize, nothing more and nothing less than a million dollars. Pilots of different nationalities will leave everything to be the champion.

Vocabulary List

- **Abandono:** Abandonment/Departure.
- **Accidente:** Accident.
- **Acelerando:** Accelerate.
- **Adelante:** Ahead.
- **Adrenalina:** Adrenaline.
- **Aficionados:** Fans.
- **Agita:** Wave/Shake.
- **Al parecer:** Apparently.
- **Árboles:** Three.
- **Argentino:** Argentine.
- **Bandera:** Flag.
- **Barrera:** Wall.
- **Batallan:** Fight/Battle.
- **Bellas:** Beautiful.
- **Bienvenido:** Welcome.
- **Brasilero:** Brazilian.
- **Calor:** Heat.
- **Cambiar:** Change.
- **Camino:** Road/Path/Way.
- **Capacidad:** Capacity.
- **Carrera:** Race/Career.
- **Cerca:** Close/Near.
- **Cerradas:** Closed.
- **Chileno:** Chilean.
- **Cielo:** Sky.
- **Cien:** A hundred.
- **Cien mil:** A hundred thousand.
- **Cincuenta mil:** Fifty thousand.
- **Cincuenta y cinco:** Fifty-five
- **Clima:** Weather.
- **Colombiano:** Colombian.
- **Comienza:** Start.
- **Cuadros:** Square.
- **Cuarenta y uno:** Forty-one.
- **Cuarto:** Four.
- **Curvas:** Turns/Curves.
- **Décimo:** Tenth.
- **Derecha:** Right.
- **Despejado:** Clear.
- **Detrás:** Behind.
- **Diecisiete:** Seventeen.
- **Emociones:** Emotions.
- **Encuentra:** Find.
- **Español:** Spanish.
- **Espera:** Wait.
- **Estadounidense:** American.
- **Fantástica:** Fantastic.
- **Frena:** Breaks.
- **Fue:** Was/Were.
- **Ganador:** Winner.
- **Gracias:** Thanks.
- **Grave:** Serious/Severe.
- **Hora:** Time/Hour.
- **Hoy:** Today.
- **Inglés:** English.
- **Intentando:** Trying.
- **Lamentablemente:** Sadly.
- **Lento:** Slow.
- **Liderato:** Lead/Leadership.
- **Llanta:** Tire.
- **Lluvia:** Rain.
- **Lugar:** Places.
- **Máxima:** Maximum.
- **Mexicano:** Mexican.
- **Mientras:** Meanwhile.
- **Montañas:** Mountains.
- **Noveno:** Ninth.
- **Nubes:** Clouds.
- **Número:** Number.
- **Ochenta:** Eighty.
- **Ocho:** Eight.
- **Octavo:** Eighth.
- **Pasar:** Pass.
- **Perfecto:** Perfect.

- **Peruano:** Peruvian.
- **Piloto:** Pilot.
- **Pista:** Track.
- **Premios:** Prizes/Awards.
- **Primer:** First.
- **Promete:** Promises.
- **Protección:** Protection/Security.
- **Próxima:** Next.
- **Quinto:** Fifth.
- **Rebasa:** Pass.
- **Rectas:** Straight lines.
- **Repentinamente:** Suddenly.
- **Riesgo:** Risk.
- **Rodeada:** Surrounded.
- **Salió:** Leave.
- **Segundo:** Second.
- **Séptimo:** Seventh.
- **Sesenta y tres:** Sixty-three.
- **Sexto:** Sixth.
- **Sigue:** Follow/Continue.
- **Sol:** Sun.
- **Tercer:** Third.
- **Toma:** Take.
- **Transmisión:** Transmission.
- **Trece:** Thirteen.
- **Treinta y nueve:** Thirty-nine.
- **Trofeos:** Trophies.
- **Un millón:** One million.
- **Vehículo:** Car.
- **Veintidós:** Twenty-two.
- **Venezolano:** Venezuelan.
- **Viento:** Wind.

Questions about the story

1. ¿Cuál es la nacionalidad es el piloto que gano la carrera?

   a. Colombiano
   b. ingles
   c. brasileño
   d. venezolano

2. ¿Cuánto fue el premio del segundo lugar?

   a. Cien mil
   b. cincuenta mil
   c. Veinte mil
   d. un millón

3. ¿Cuál era el número del piloto que partió de primer lugar?

   a. Sesenta y tres
   b. ocho
   c. cincuenta y cinco
   d. trece

4. ¿Cuál fue la posición en la que llego el piloto venezolano?

   a. Segundo
   b. primero
   c. tercero
   d. ninguna de las anteriores

5. ¿Cuántos pilotos participaron en la carrera?

   a. Doce
   b. catorce
   c. ocho
   d. ninguna de las anteriores

Answers

1. C - What is the nationality of the driver who won the race?
2. D - How much was the second place prize?
3. D - What was the number of the pilot who started first?
4. A - What was the position in which the Venezuelan pilot finished?
5. D - How many pilots participated in the race?

Chapter Six

Basic Nouns

Un caballo valiente / A Brave Horse

Nick era un **empresario** exitoso, **dueño** de una **empresa** muy importante. Un **día** comenzó un **incendio** en el **edificio** donde trabajaba, quedando atrapado en su **oficina**. Toda la oficina se llenó de **humo** y Nick solo podía ver **llamas** a su alrededor. Una gran **viga** cayó encima de él. Nick pensó que moriría allí, pero afortunadamente los **bomberos** lo encontraron. Nick fue llevado al **hospital** con algunas **quemaduras** graves. Cuando se recuperó y fue dado de alta se fue a su **casa**, pero luego de un tiempo todo cambió. Se sentía muy diferente, fue difícil para él, ya que al salir a la **calle** tenía **ataques de ansiedad** y sufría de **pesadillas** constantes. Busco **ayuda** en su **hermana**, ella era la persona que él más quería, ella ayudó a buscar **métodos** para poder superar la situación que él vivía.

Luego de ir a varios **doctores**, diagnosticaron que Nick sufría de trastorno de estrés postraumático (PTSD). Después de investigar, Nick y su hermana descubrieron una **terapia** alternativa muy efectiva con **caballos**. Nick estaba cansado de sufrir esta **enfermedad**, así que aceptó hacer esta terapia y fue a un bello y gran **rancho** donde tienen caballos especiales que ayudan a las personas que sufren de esta y otro tipo de enfermedades **similares**.

Adam era el **encargado** del rancho y quien dirigía las **terapias**. Un **día** recibió a Nick y lo llevó a conocer a quien sería su mejor **amigo** y quien le ayudaría a recuperarse, le llevó a un **establo** donde estaba un caballo hermoso pura **sangre** de **pelo** marrón oscuro, **patas** largas torneadas y una **cola** muy frondosa. Su nombre era **valiente**.

Adam le contó que el nombre es porque cuando era un **potro** salvó a la **hija** de Adam de ahogarse. Nick se sintió desde el primer **momento** conectado con el caballo, juntos comenzaron la terapia. Nick tuvo que aprender a confiar en el caballo y el caballo en Nick. Poco a poco se fueron encariñando, Nick fue superando todos los **miedos** y malos **recuerdos** que tenía.

Después de terminar su terapia había hecho una **conexión** tan grande con valiente que decidió quedarse trabajando en el rancho. Así estar junto a su mejor amigo y poder ayudar a otras personas que lo necesiten.

Resumen de la historia

Nick quien es un empresario exitoso tenía todo lo que podía desear, lamentablemente un día un incendio que se produjo en su edificio cambió radicalmente su vida. Nick vio la muerte muy cerca. Luego de haber estado en el hospital con quemaduras graves, al salir para él todo cambió, comenzó a sufrir pesadillas y ansiedad. Fue diagnosticado con Trastorno de estrés postraumático, pero con la ayuda de un caballo valiente podrá seguir continuar y recuperar su vida.

Summary of the story

Nick is a successful businessman who had everything he could wish. Unfortunately, one day a fire that broke out in his building radically changed his life. Nick saw death very close. After being in the hospital with severe burns, when he got out, everything changed for him. He began to suffer from nightmares and anxiety. He was diagnosed with Post Traumatic Stress Disorder, but with the help of a brave horse, he will be able to go on and get his life back.

Vocabulary List (Nouns)

- **Adam:** Adam.
- **Amigo:** Friend.
- **Ayuda:** Help.
- **Ataque de ansiedad:** Anxiety attack.
- **Bomberos:** Firefighters.
- **Casa:** House.
- **Caballos:** Horses.
- **Cola:** Tail.
- **Conexión:** Connection.
- **Día:** Day.
- **Doctores:** Doctors/Medics. (Plural)
- **Dueño:** Owner.
- **Edificio:** Building.
- **Empresa:** Company.
- **Empresario:** Businessman
- **Encargado:** Manager.
- **Enfermedad:** Sickness.
- **Establo:** Stable.
- **Hermana:** Sister.
- **Hija:** Daugther.
- **Hospital:** Hospital.
- **Humo:** Smoke.
- **Incendio:** Fire/Blaze.
- **Llamas:** Flames.
- **Métodos:** Methods. (Plural)
- **Miedos:** Fears. (Plural)
- **Momento:** Moment.
- **Nick:** Nick.
- **Oficina:** Office.
- **Patas:** Legs. (Plural)
- **Pelo:** Hair.
- **Persona:** Person.
- **Pesadillas:** Nightmares. (Plural)
- **Potro:** Colt.
- **Quemaduras:** Burns.
- **Rancho:** Ranch.
- **Sangre:** Blood.
- **Situaciones:** Situations.
- **Terapia:** Therapy.
- **Terapias:** Therapies.
- **Valiente:** Brave. (Proper name)
- **Viga:** Beam.

Questions about the story

1. ¿Por qué fue a terapia Nick?

    a. Porque terminó una relación amorosa.
    b. Porque tenía pesadillas.
    c. Porque tenía problemas de ira.
    d. Ninguna de las anteriores.

2. ¿Cómo se llama el encargado del rancho?

    a. Dan
    b. Víctor
    c. Nick
    d. Adam

3. ¿A quién salvó el caballo en la historia?

    a. La esposa de Adam.
    b. La mamá de Adam.
    c. La hija de Adam.
    d. Un trabajador del rancho.

4. ¿Cuál era la profesión de nick?

    a. Militar.
    b. Bombero .
    c. Cajero de banco.
    d. Empresario.

5. ¿Qué sucedió en el edificio donde trabajaba Nick?

    a. Un incendio.
    b. Una inundación
    c. Un sismo.
    d. Ninguna de las anteriores.

Answers

1. B - Why did Nick go to therapy?
2. D - What is the ranch manager's name?
3. C - Who did the horse save in the story?
4. D - What was Nick's profession?
5. A - What happened in the building where Nick worked?

Chapter Seven

Basic Vocabulary. (Food)

Cocinando con la abuela/ Cooking With Grandma

Óscar y Viviana estaban muy felices, pues iban de **visita** a ver a su **abuela** Carmen. Que siempre les preparaba **ricas comidas, saladas** y **dulces**. Al llegar salieron del carro y entraron a la **cocina**, donde estaba su abuela esperándolos.

"Llegaron mis nietos ¡qué alegría! ¿Cómo están?" dice la abuela Carmen.

"Estamos muy bien abuela. ¿Dinos que **plato** nos prepararas hoy?" dijeron los niños.

"Hoy no solo les voy a **cocinar**, hoy les voy a enseñar cómo **preparar diversos platillos** extremadamente **deliciosos**", dice la abuela Carmen feliz porque sus nietos la visitaron.

Así comenzaron a preparar la cocina, **colocando** todos los **utensilios** que pensaban **utilizar**, como **cuchillos, cucharas, tenedores, platos, ollas** y **sartenes**. Luego empezaron a cocinar. Su abuela busca en unas **gavetas** saca algo y les dice a los niños:

"Muy bien, aquí tenemos los **delantales** para convertirnos en todos unos **cocineros**".

Comenzaron preparando una **lasaña deliciosa**. Óscar fue el encargado de traer los **ingredientes**, los cuales eran: **aceite, tocino, carne, tomate, sal, pimientos, pimienta, zanahoria, cebolla, champiñones, pasta, salsa de tomate, queso**.

"Muy bien, primero ponemos la sartén", dice la abuela explicando la **preparación**.

Comenzaron echando el aceite, luego **picaron** el tocino en **cubos** y la **colocaron** en la sartén a **fuego medio**. Picaron las **verduras**, las zanahorias, las cebollas, pimientos y los champiñones. **Echaron** la carne, la sal y la pimienta en la sartén. Con los tomates hicieron un **puré**, la cual combinaron con la preparación. De último **vertieron** la salsa de tomate y todo lo cocinaron. El siguiente paso fue cocinar las **capas** de la lasaña. Primero **colocaron** una capa de pasta **previamente cocida**, luego colocaron una capa de carne y **repitieron** varias veces este proceso. Al finalizar la última capa era de **queso**, y la **llevaron** al **horno** hasta que el queso **gratinara**.

"Ahora prepararemos la **ensalada** con **huevo**", dice la abuela mientras busca todos los ingredientes.

Ellos buscan los siguientes ingredientes: **papa**, zanahoria, **cilantro**, huevo, **aceite de oliva, mayonesa, guisantes y limón**. Comienzan **pelando** las papas y las zanahorias, las pican en cubos **pequeños** y las cocinan con **agua**. Los huevos se cocinan **aparte** en agua hasta que **hiervan**. Una vez que la papa y la zanahoria se ablanden se llevan a un **bol**. Los huevos se sacan del agua, se les **quita** la **cáscara** y se pican en cubos también. Luego **mezclan** los huevos con la papa y la zanahoria. Se **agregan** los guisantes, con dos **cucharadas** de mayonesa, una cucharada de aceite de oliva, un poco de **zumo** de limón, y sal. Se mezcla todo y al final pican cilantro y se vierte en la mezcla para darle **frescura**.

"Luego de la ensalada prepararemos unas deliciosas **pechugas de pollo**, con **salsa agridulce** y **arroz**", dice la abuela emocionada.

Ellos buscan: pechuga de pollo, **ajo**, sal, pimienta, aceite de oliva, limón. Para la **salsa** necesitan: **vinagre, salsa de soja, azúcar, maicena**, agua, salsa de tomate, y **orégano**. La preparación comienza **lavando** la pechuga con agua y zumo de limón, luego se le agrega la sal, la pimienta y un ajo **triturado**. En una sartén se vierte el vinagre, la salsa de soja, la salsa de tomate, el azúcar. Se **revuelve** hasta que **espese** y se coloca la pechuga **picada** en cubos. Luego se mezcla agua con maicena y se **vierte** en la preparación. Por último, se agrega el orégano y se **sirve acompañada** del arroz.

"Por último queda preparar el **postre**, haremos unas **ricas** y **sencillas galletas**", dice la abuela mientras se prepara para seguir cocinando.

Para esta receta van a usar: **harina**, azúcar, **mantequilla, vainilla, leche** y **chispas de chocolate**. En un bol **colocarán** la leche, la mantequilla **derretida previamente**, el azúcar, la harina y un **toque** de vainilla. Se mezcla todo hasta **lograr** una **masa consistente**. Después se lleva a la **nevera** por quince minutos, la **sacan** y la **extienden**. La **cortan** con pequeños **moldes**. La colocan en una **bandeja** mientras le **agregan** chispas de chocolate por **encima**. Se lleva al horno hasta que estén **doradas**.

"Muy bien niños, ¡gran trabajo!", dice la abuela "es hora de **poner** la **mesa**".

Todos se sentaron a **comer** los platos deliciosos, los cuales la abuela y los niños prepararon.

Resumen de la historia

Carmen es una abuela dulce que le gusta mucho cocinar para su familia. Es una amante de la cocina, y un día que sus nietos llegan de visita, Carmen ve la oportunidad de transmitir el conocimiento culinario a sus nietos amados. Los niños felices de poder cocinar con su abuela, ellos prepararon platillos deliciosos y sobre todo hechos con mucho amor.

Summary of the story

Carmen is a sweet grandmother who loves to cook for her family. She is a lover of cooking, and one day when her grandchildren come to visit, Carmen sees the opportunity to pass on her culinary knowledge to her beloved grandchildren. The children were happy to cook with their grandmother. They prepared delicious dishes and above all made with lots of love.

Vocabulary List

- **Abuela:** Grandmother.
- **Aceite:** Oil.
- **Aceite de oliva:** Olive oil.
- **Acompañada:** Accompanied.
- **Agregan:** Add.
- **Agua:** Water.
- **Ajo:** Garlic.
- **Aparte:** Aside/Apart.
- **Arroz:** Rice.
- **Azúcar:** Sugar.
- **Bandeja:** Tray.
- **Bol:** Bowl.
- **Capas:** layers.
- **Carne:** Meat.
- **Cáscara:** Shell.
- **Cebolla:** Onion.
- **Champiñones:** Mushrooms. (Plural)
- **Chispas de chocolate:** Chocolate chips. (Plural)
- **Cilantro:** Coriander.
- **Cocida:** Cocida.
- **Cocina:** Kitchen.
- **Cocinar:** Cook.
- **Cocineros:** Chefs. (Plural)
- **Colocando:** Placing/Putting.
- **Comer:** Eat.
- **Comidas:** Food/Meals. (Plural)
- **Consistente:** Consistent.
- **Cortan:** Cut.
- **Cubos:** Cubes.(Plural)
- **Cucharadas:** Spoonfuls. (Plural)
- **Cucharas:** Spoons. (Plural)
- **Cuchillos:** Knifes.
- **Delantales:** Apron.
- **Deliciosa:** Delicious.
- **Derretida:** Melted.
- **Diversos:** Diverse/Various.
- **Doradas:** Golden/Golden brown.
- **Dulces:** Sweet.
- **Echaron:** Pour.
- **Encima:** On/On top.
- **Ensalada:** Salad.
- **Espese:** Thicken.
- **Extienden:** Extend/Spread/Roll out.
- **Frescura:** Fresh.

- **Fuego:** Fire/Heat.
- **Galletas:** Cookies. (Plural)
- **Gavetas:** Drawers.
- **Gratinará:** Au gratin/Witch cheese.
- **Guisantes:** Peas.
- **Harina:** Flour.
- **Hiervan:** Boil.
- **Horno:** Oven.
- **Huevo:** Egg.
- **Ingredientes:** Ingredients.
- **Lasaña:** Lasagna.
- **Lavando:** Washing/Cleaning.
- **Leche:** Milk.
- **Limón:** Lemon.
- **Llevaron:** They took.
- **Lograr:** Achieve/Make.
- **Maicena:** Cornstarch
- **Mantequilla:** Butter.
- **Masa:** Dough/Mass.
- **Mayonesa:** Mayonnaise.
- **Medio:** Middle.
- **Mesa:** Table.
- **Mezclan:** Mix/Blend.
- **Moldes:** Molds.
- **Nevera:** Fridge.
- **Ollas:** Pots/Pans.
- **Orégano:** Oregano.
- **Papa:** Potato.
- **Pasta:** Pasta.
- **Pechugas:** Breasts.
- **Pelando:** Peeling.
- **Pequeños:** Little/Small.
- **Picada:** Chopped.
- **Picaron:** Chopped.
- **Pimienta:** Pepper.
- **Pimientos:** Peppers.
- **Platillos:** Dishes/Plates.
- **Plato:** Plate.
- **Pollo:** Chiken.
- **Poner:** Put/Place/Set.

- **Postre:** Dessert.
- **Preparación:** Preparation.
- **Preparar:** Prepare.
- **Previamente:** Previously.
- **Proceso:** Process.
- **Puré:** Puree.
- **Queso:** Cheese.
- **Quita:** Remove.
- **Repitieron:** They repeated.
- **Revuelve:** Scramble.
- **Ricas.** Tasty.
- **Sacan:** Take out.
- **Sal:** Salt.
- **Saladas:** Salty.
- **Salsa:** Sauce.
- **Salsa agridulce:** Sweet and sour sauce.
- **Salsa de soja:** Soy sauce.
- **Salsa de tomate:** Ketchup.
- **Sartenes:** Frying pans.
- **Sencillas:** Easy.
- **Sirve:** Serve.
- **Tenedores:** Forks. (Plural)
- **Tocineta:** Bacon.
- **Tomate:** Tomato.
- **Toque:** Touch.
- **Triturado:** Shredded.
- **Utensilios:** Utensils/Tools. (Plural)
- **Utilizar:** Use.
- **Vainilla:** Vanilla.
- **Verduras:** Vegetables.
- **Vierte:** Pour/Spill.
- **Vinagre:** Vinegar.
- **Visita:** Visit.
- **Zanahoria:** Carrot.
- **Zumo:** Juice.

Questions about the story

1. ¿Cuántas recetas prepararon en la historia?

    a. Cinco.
    b. Cuatro.
    c. Tres.
    d. Dos.

2. ¿Cómo se llama la abuela?

    a. María.
    b. Juana.
    c. Carmen.
    d. Ninguna de las anteriores.

3. ¿Qué sabor tenían las galletas que prepararon?

    a. Canela.
    b. Vainilla.
    c. Limón.
    d. Chocolate.

4. ¿Quiénes eran los niños de la historia?

    a. Los nietos.
    b. Los sobrinos.
    c. Los hijos.
    d. Ninguna de las anteriores.

5. ¿Cuál fue el primer plato que cocinaron?

    a. Galletas.
    b. Ensalada.
    c. Pollo.
    d. Lasaña.

Answers

1. **C - How many recipes did they prepare in history?**
2. **C - What is the grandmother's name?**
3. **D - What was the flavor of the cookies they made?**
4. **A - Who were the children in the story?**
5. **D - What was the first dish you cooked?**

Chapter Eight

Basic Vocabulary

Conquistar la tierra/Conquer the Land

Mi nombre es Einar, soy un joven que vive en las **inmensas** montañas de Escandinavia. Mi padre me llamo así pues este nombre **significa líder guerrero**, y para eso me **criaron** y **educaron**. Nací en Wilhelm, en un pequeño **reino** nórdico, donde mi padre me **entrenó** desde pequeño para **triunfar** y ser un gran líder guerrero del **ejército** del **rey**, lugar que mi padre ocupaba, **aprendí** a **cazar** y a **pelear**. Soy un **experto** en **batalla** con **espada**, el mejor **arquero**, el más rápido, **sigiloso**, fuerte y **ágil** de todos. A los veinte años, ocupe mi lugar en el ejército del rey Ulfric. Tengo a **trescientos** hombres a mi **mando**, todos me **respetan** y sé que algunos hasta me **temen**.

Hoy el rey **celebra** un **banquete** para mí y mis hombres, ya que mañana saldremos a batalla. Tenemos la **orden** de viajar al reino cercano a **conquistarlo** y **expulsar** a los **invasores**, para recuperar nuestro **territorio**. Actualmente vivimos una **guerra** civil, ya que ese imperio invasor nos ha prohibido **adorar** a nuestros dioses. Realmente yo no quiero ir a ese banquete, prefiero **quedarme** en mi hogar y **descansar** para la batalla que nos espera, pero el rey solicitó mi **presencia**, por lo cual tengo que ir aunque no quiera. Llegue y no me gusto lo que vi, todos mis **soldados** están casi **borrachos**, **bebiendo cerveza**, **riendo** y **comiendo**; hay mujeres y música, me parece la **escena** más **absurda** e **incoherente**. Mañana **partiremos** a batalla y mis hombres deberían estar descansando, **mentalizándose** para lo que nos espera mañana.

Mientras veo todo esto, estoy **sumergido** en mis **pensamientos**. El rey Ulfric me pone una mano en mi **espalda** y me dice que espera mañana tener un reino más en sus **manos**; yo solo le sonrió y le digo que no se preocupe que así será, pero en mi **interior** me cuestiono ¿cómo **ganaremos** si todos mis hombres mañana estarán con los **estragos** de esta noche?, el rey se va a atender a otras personas y quedó de nuevo solo; pensando en como mañana les pondré un **castigo** a mis hombres, ya que no es posible que al saber que mañana tienen un **deber** que **cumplir**, hoy están bebiendo.

Sé que la mayoría de guerreros la noche antes de una gran batalla beben y comen como si no hubiera mañana, pero esto a mí me parece un pensamiento

inútil. Si yo viese este día como mi último día, seguro mañana muera en el campo de batalla y no **pretendo** que esto suceda.

Mientras pienso en todo esto, la veo a ella, tan hermosa, **pura** y **celestial**. Amelia, la **hija** del rey, mi mayor y único amor a quien he contemplado y admirado desde el primer día que la vi. Desde niños nos **enamoramos**, y este amor creció al pasar de los años. Cuando termine con mi misión, pretendo **pedirle la mano** a la **princesa** Amelia. Luego de un largo rato el banquete acaba, yo me voy a mi hogar no sin antes decirles a mis hombres que vayan directo a descansar, ya que mañana le espera mucho que hacer.

Pero no puedo **dormir, asumiendo** que mi **enemigo** estará más preparado y en mejores **condiciones**, empiezo a crear una **estrategia** que nos permita ganar este territorio. En vez de **atacar directamente, planeó** atacar por los **costados** y **acorralar** a mi enemigo hasta el **puente** del dragón, esta es la única entrada para llegar a Solitude, allí ganaría acceso para llegar al **castillo** y lograr la victoria. Salgo de mi pequeña **cabaña**, preparándome para **partir rumbo** a Solitude, pero antes de irme paso a ver a Amelia, le **prometo** que al volver le diré a su padre que la amo y que quiero que sea mi **esposa**.

Al llegar a Solitude, nos esperaba el ejército del rey Torygg. Mis hombres comienzan a batallar y aunque nos **duplican** en número, mi estrategia funciona. Mis hombres son guerreros nórdicos criados para la batalla. La **presión** de nuestro ejército es tan grande que **logramos avanzar, observando** a mi **alrededor detecto** que los soldados del rey Torygg se están **retirando**, y cuando estamos a punto de llegar al puente del dragón, es en este momento que empiezo a **saborear** la victoria, pero **de repente** siento un frío **golpe** en el **pecho**, tan frío como el metal. Solo logro ver a Amelia y sus bellos ojos azules esperándome en el Valhalla.

Resumen de la historia

La historia de Einar comienza cuando un joven nórdico nos cuenta cómo su padre le entrena para ser un guerrero desde que era un niño. Einar era el hijo del líder del ejército del rey Ulfric. Sigue los pasos de su padre, convirtiéndose en el nuevo líder de ese poderoso ejército. A los veinte años, se convierte en el líder de trescientos hombres que le respetan e incluso le temen. Einar nos cuenta cómo él y sus hombres pasan la noche antes de la gran batalla para conquistar Soledad y cómo en esta guerra. Cuando estuvo cerca de la victoria en la batalla tristemente termina herido, y muere imaginando los ojos de su amada.

Summary of the story

The story of Einar begins when a young Nordic boy tells us how his father trains him to be a warrior since he was a child. Einar was the son of the leader of King Ulfric's army. He follows the steps of his father, becoming the new leader of that powerful army. At the age of twenty, he becomes the leader of three hundred men who respect and even fear him. Einar tells us how he and his men spend the night before the great battle to conquer Solitude and how in this war. When he was close to victory in battle sadly ends up wounded, and dying imaging the eyes of his beloved.

Vocabulary List

- **Absurda:** Absurd.
- **Acorralar:** Corner.
- **Adorar:** Worship.
- **Ágil:** Agile.
- **Alrededor:** Around.
- **Aprendí:** I learned.
- **Arquero:** Archer.
- **Asumiendo:** Assuming.
- **Atacar:** Attack.
- **Avanzar:** Move Forward/ Progress/Move on.
- **Banquete:** Banquet/Feast.
- **Batalla:** Battle.
- **Bebiendo:** Drinking.
- **Borrachos:** Drunk.
- **Cabaña:** Cabin.
- **Castigo:** Punishment.
- **Castillo:** Castle.
- **Cazar:** Hunt.
- **Celebra:** Celebrate.
- **Celestial:** Celestial.
- **Cerveza:** Beer.
- **Comiendo:** Eating.
- **Condiciones:** Conditions.
- **Conquistarlo:** Conquer it.
- **Costados:** Sides/Flanks. (Plural)
- **Criaron:** Raised.
- **Cumplir:** Fulfil/Meet/Comply.
- **De repente:** Suddenly.
- **Deber:** Duty.
- **Descansar:** Rest.
- **Detecto:** Detect.
- **Directamente:** Directly.
- **Dormir:** Sleep.
- **Duplican:** Double.
- **Educaron:** Educate.
- **Ejército:** Army.
- **Enamoramos:** In love.
- **Enemigo:** Enemy.
- **Entrenó:** Trained.
- **Escena:** Scene.
- **Espada:** Sword.
- **Esposa:** Wife.
- **Estragos:** Havoc/Ravages.
- **Estrategia:** Strategy.
- **Experto:** Expert.
- **Expulsar:** Expel.
- **Ganaremos:** We will win.
- **Golpe:** Hit/Blow.
- **Guerra:** War.
- **Guerrero:** Warrior.
- **Hija:** Daughter.

- **Incoherente:** Incoherent.
- **Inmensas:** Immense.
- **Interior:** Inside/Interior.
- **Inútil:** Useless.
- **Invasores:** Invaders.
- **Líder:** Leader.
- **Logramos:** Succeeded.
- **Mando:** Command/Control.
- **Manos:** Hands.
- **Mentalizándose:** Mentalizing.
- **Observando:** Observing.
- **Orden:** Order/Command.
- **Partir rumbo:** Departure.
- **Partiremos:** We will leave.
- **Pecho:** Chest.
- **Pedirle la mano:** Asking for her hand/ Marriage proposal.
- **Pelear:** Figth.
- **Pensamientos:** Thoughts.
- **Planeó:** Planned.
- **Presencia:** Presence.
- **Presión:** Pressure.
- **Pretendo:** Pretend.
- **Princesa:** Princess.
- **Prometo:** I promise.
- **Puente:** Bridge.
- **Pura:** Pure.
- **Quedarme:** Stay.
- **Reino:** Kingdom.
- **Respetan:** Respect.
- **Retirando:** Retreating/Withdrawing.
- **Rey:** King.
- **Riendo:** Laughing.
- **Saborear:** Taste.
- **Sigiloso:** Stealthy.
- **Significa:** Meaning.
- **Soldados:** Soldiers.
- **Sumergido:** Submerged/Immersed.
- **Temen:** Fear.
- **Territorio:** Territory.
- **Trescientos:** Three hundred.
- **Triunfar:** Succeed.

Questions about the story

1. ¿Quién fue el último líder del ejército del rey?

    a.   Ulfric.
    b.   Torygg.
    c.   Einar.
    d.   Beowulf.

2. ¿Cómo se llama la hija del rey?

    a.   Melina.
    b.   Amelia.
    c.   Idra.
    d.   Freya.

3. ¿Para qué entrenaron a Einar?

    a.   Para ser rey.
    b.   Para ser esposo de la hija del rey.
    c.   Para ser líder del ejército.
    d.   Ninguna de las anteriores.

4. ¿Cuántos hombres conformaban el ejército?

    a.   Quinientos.
    b.   Seiscientos.
    c.   Doscientos.
    d.   Trescientos.

5. ¿Cuál era la misión del ejército?

    a.   Conquistar Wilhelm.
    b.   Conquistar Solitude.
    c.   Matar a un dragón.
    d.   Matar al rey.

Answers

1. C - Who was the last leader of the king's army?
2. B - What is the name of the king's daughter?
3. C - What was Einar trained for?
4. D - How many men made up the army?
5. B - What was the mission of the army?

Chapter Nine

Basic Nouns

Problemas en la montaña/Trouble in the Mountain

Alejandro, Jorge, Alan, Sebastián y Camila eran cinco **amigos** que un **día** decidieron que la mejor **actividad** en unas **vacaciones** era acampar, siendo Alan, Camila y Sebastián quienes eran los **campistas** experimentados, mientras que para Alejandro y Jorge sería su **primera vez**. Todos ellos eran amigos desde hace mucho **tiempo** y en una reunión todos se pusieron de acuerdo para ir.

El **destino** que eligieron fue la **montaña Lomas** del **Viento**, la montaña más alta de la **región**. Para llegar a ella hay que viajar y caminar varios **kilómetros**. Los **muchachos** llegaron hasta un **punto** en **autobús**, luego pidieron **aventón**, un peculiar **lugareño** en su **camioneta** los recogió, todos se montaron pensando que no pasaría nada, pero estaban muy equivocados. Este lugareño condujo como loco por la **carretera**, giraba a gran **velocidad** en las **curvas**. Los pobres muchachos estaban aterrados moviéndose de un **lado** al otro, y a pesar de los **gritos** el **conductor** no disminuía la velocidad. El conductor se detiene bruscamente en la **base** de la montaña para que los **campistas** se bajen y continúen su **camino**, al reclamarle este les dijo que era una **broma** y por eso acelero, que lo disculparan.

Los campistas molestos se despidieron y continuaron su camino ascendiendo la montaña. Todo lucia hermoso, mientras caminaban se encontraban con muchas **piedras**, **árboles** largos con **frutos**, de **madera** robusta y con **troncos** anchos; las **flores** eran delicadas y coloridas; las **nubes** eran claras y el **sol** resplandecía. Se escuchaban muchos **sonidos** como el de la **tierra** al ser **pisada**, el de **aves**, **venados**, **perros** e **insectos**. Los campistas estaban contentos mientras contemplaban la **naturaleza**, hablaban, contaban **anécdotas** y uno que otro **chiste**. Por andar distraídos empezaron a caminar en **círculos**, debido a esto empezaron a trabajar en **equipo** para encontrar otra vez la **ruta**. Finalmente consiguieron un **río**, con **agua** dulce y cristalina. Se podían ver a numerosos **peces** nadando en estas aguas.

Todos recargaron sus **cantimploras** y **contenedores** continuando su camino. Sin darse cuenta llegaron a la **cima**, todos contentos se sentaron a contemplar el **paisaje**. Instalaron el **campamento** y todo lucia genial, comieron y jugaron toda la **tarde**. Alrededor de las cuatro de la tarde empezaron a recoger **leña** para hacer la **fogata**, pero cuando fueron a buscar la madera, se dieron cuenta de que el **piso** estaba mojado y resbaladizo, y por ello se caían a cada **rato**. Llego la **noche** y todo era perfecto, la **luna** brillaba y el **cielo** estaba lleno de **estrellas**. Luego de cenar fueron a dormir y fue una buena noche.

A la **mañana** siguiente se despertaron con un bello paisaje, el sol recién salía, las nubes lucían como **algodón**, el cielo era azul y cálido. A lo lejos escucharon a los **pájaros** cantar, todo era como un **retrato** hermoso. Se sentía una **paz** y tranquilidad incomparable. Ese día si pudieron recolectar madera seca que consiguieron en el **bosque**, también buscaron frutos y más agua. Cantaron, contaron **historias** de **terror**, asaron **malvaviscos** y **salchichas** al rededor del **fuego** y se divirtieron como nunca. Hasta que llego la noche, las nubes se oscurecieron y **truenos** empezaron a escucharse cerca; y de repente empezó a llover muy intensamente. Todos los **chicos** entraron a sus respectivas **carpas**, pero la **tormenta** era tan fuerte que el agua comenzó a entrar en estas. Solo una estaba seca, y era la carpa de Alan así que Alejandro, Camila, Sebastián y Jorge entraron a esta para resguardarse de la **lluvia**, todas sus **pertenecías** se mojaron. Esa noche fue muy incómoda para ellos, eran cinco en una pequeña carpa para uno, solo algunos pudieron dormir, ya que tenían mucho **miedo** a que la carpa fallara y se destruyera, aunque las **risas** no faltaron.

La lluvia cesó a la mañana siguiente, todos salieron muy maltratados y con mucho **sueño**, ya que casi ni durmieron, muchas de sus pertenencias quedaron inservibles o se perdieron. Debido a esta situación decidieron regresarse a **casa**, aunque parezca una mala **experiencia** la realidad es que todos estaban increíblemente felices, ya que a pesar de las **dificultades** todos vivieron una experiencia única que siempre van a recordar y que sin duda volverían a repetirla.

Resumen de la historia

Este grupo de amigos decidieron que la mejor actividad que podían hacer en sus vacaciones era ir de campamento. Algunos tenían bastante experiencia, los otros eran totales inexpertos en este mundo. Desde el comienzo de su viaje vivieron un sin fin de situaciones inesperadas y extremadamente peligrosas que los pusieron aprueba. A pesar de todas las dificultades que enfrentaron, terminaron amando esta experiencia.

Summary of the story

This group of friends decided that the best activity they could do on their vacation was to go camping. Some of them were quite experienced, and the others were inexperienced in this world. From the very beginning of their trip, they experienced an endless number of unexpected and extremely dangerous situations that put them to the test. Despite all the difficulties they faced, they ended up loving the experience.

Vocabulary List

- **Actividad:** Activity.
- **Agua:** Water.
- **Algodón:** Cotton.
- **Amigos:** Friends. (Plural)
- **Anécdotas:** Anecdotes. (Plural)
- **Árboles:** Trees. (Plural)
- **Autobús:** Bus. (Plural)
- **Aventón:** Ride/Lift.
- **Aves:** Birds. (Plural)
- **Base:** Base.
- **Bosque:** Forest
- **Broma:** Joke/Prank.
- **Camino:** Road/Way/Path.
- **Camioneta:** Truck.
- **Campamento:** Camp.
- **Campistas:** Campers. (Plural)
- **Cantimploras:** Canteens. (Plural)
- **Carpas:** Tents. (Plural)
- **Carretera:** Road/Route.
- **Casa:** House.
- **Chicos:** Guys/Boys/Folks.(Plural)
- **Chiste:** Joke.
- **Cielo:** Sky.
- **Cima:** Top.
- **Círculos:** Circles.
- **Conductor:** Driver.
- **Contenedores:** Containers. (Plural)
- **Curvas:** Turns/Curves (Plural)
- **Destino:** Destination/Destiny.
- **Día:** Day.
- **Dificultades:** Difficulties. (Plural)
- **Equipo:** Team/Crew.
- **Estrellas:** Stars. (Plural)
- **Experiencia:** Experience.
- **Flores:** Flowers. (Plural)
- **Fogata:** Bonfire.
- **Frutos:** Fruits. (Plural)
- **Fuego:** Fire.
- **Gritos:** Screams. (Plural)
- **Historias:** Stories. (Plural)
- **Insectos:** Insects. (Plural)
- **Kilómetros:** Kilometers. (Plural)
- **Lado:** Side.
- **Leña:** Firewood.
- **Lomas:** Hills. (Plural)
- **Lluvia:** Rain.
- **Lugareño:** Local.
- **Luna:** Moon.
- **Madera:** Wood.
- **Malvaviscos:** Marshmallows. (Plural)
- **Mañana:** Tomorrow/Morning.
- **Miedo:** Fear.
- **Montaña:** Mountain.
- **Muchachos:** Guys. (Plural)
- **Naturaleza:** Nature.

- **Noche:** Night.
- **Nubes:** Clouds. (Plural)
- **Paisaje:** Landscape.
- **Pájaros:** Birds. (Plural)
- **Paz:** Peace.
- **Peces:** Fishes. (Plural)
- **Perros:** Dogs. (Plural)
- **Pertenecías:** Belongings. (Plural)
- **Piedras:** Rocks. (Plural)
- **Pisada:** Footprint.
- **Piso:** Floor.
- **Punto:** Point.
- **Rato:** While.
- **Región:** Region.
- **Retrato:** Portrait.
- **Río:** River.
- **Risas:** Laugh. (Plural)
- **Ruta:** Track/Route.
- **Salchichas:** Sausages. (Plural)
- **Sol:** Sun.
- **Sonidos:** Sounds. (Plural)
- **Sueño:** Dreams/Goals.
- **Tarde:** Afternoon/Late.
- **Terror:** Terror.
- **Tiempo:** Weather.
- **Tierra:** Earth/Land/Soil/Dirt.
- **Tormenta:** Storm.
- **Troncos:** Trunks. (Plural)
- **Truenos:** Tunders/Lightnings. (Plural)
- **Vacaciones:** Vacations. (Plural)
- **Velocidad:** Speed.
- **Venados:** Deers. (Plural)
- **Viento:** Wind.

Questions about the story

1. ¿Cómo se llama la montaña en la que acamparon?

    a. Montaña del viento.

    b. Lomas de la Montaña.

    c. Lomas del viento.

    d. Viento de Montaña.

2. ¿Quiénes eran los campistas novatos?

    a. Alejandro y Jorge.

    b. Alan y Camila.

    c. Sebastián y Alejandro.

    d. Alan y Jorge.

3. ¿Cómo llegaron los campistas a la base de la montaña?

    a. En autobús.

    b. En tren.

    c. En aventón.

    d. Caminando.

4. ¿Qué ayudo a los campistas cuando estaban perdidos?

    a. Un rio.

    b. Un arbol.

    c. Una roca.

    d. Ninguna de las anteriores.

5. ¿Qué sucedió en la última noche?

    a. Una lluvia fuerte.

    b. Nada.

    c. Un terremoto.

    d. Unos animales atacaron el campamento.

Answers

1. **C** - What is the name of the mountain where they camped?
2. **A** - Who were the rookie campers?
3. **C** - How did the campers get to the base of the mountain?
4. **A** - What helped the campers when they were lost?
5. **A** - What happened on the last night?

Chapter Ten

Basic Vocabulary

Tocando por un sueño/Playing for a Dream

Carlos era un niño de once años, muy **lindo** y **tranquilo**, que vivía con su abuela y su papá. Su papá era **dueño** de un **taller mecánico**, y desde que Carlos era pequeño su padre siempre le dijo que él tendría que **hacerse** cargo del **negocio** cuando **creciera**. Pero el **sueño** de Carlos era otro, él quería ser **músico**, siendo su actividad favorita tocar la **guitarra** y el **piano**.

Aprendió a **tocar** y a **cantar** gracias a su **vecino**, un **viejo bohemio** quien nunca tuvo **hijos**, y al ver en el niño un **interés** por la música le quiso enseñar todos sus **conocimientos** musicales. Su nombre es Francisco, él es un músico que por mucho tiempo fue parte de un gran **grupo** de mariachis. Estos eran muy **conocidos** y **populares** en su país. Le contaba **anécdotas** al pequeño Carlos de cómo viajó por el mundo tocando su música. **Tristemente** Francisco nunca tuvo hijos, y es la razón por la cual Francisco le **agarró cariño** al pequeño Carlos, él **deseaba** tener hijos para poder un día **enseñarles** a tocar **instrumentos**.Carlos desde muy pequeño sintió una **atracción** a la música, cada vez que su abuela **encendía** la radio, el pequeño Carlos **bailaba** y **cantaba**. A la edad de seis años su abuela le **regaló** una pequeña guitarra **pensando** que esto solo sería un pequeño **pasatiempo**. Lo que ella nunca supo era que al regalarle esa guitarra, Carlos había **encontrado** su **verdadera pasión**. Muchas veces a Carlos le gustaba salir a la **acera** de su casa para tocar con la guitarra, y así fue que Francisco **descubrió** el **talento** en el joven Carlos.

Lo **lamentable** era que al padre de Carlos no le gustaba que su hijo **pasara** tanto tiempo con el músico. Su papá le decía que la música no le daría para vivir, que era un sueño **absurdo** y que él tenía que seguir el trabajo de la familia. Por esta razón le **prohibió** a Carlos seguir **yendo** a clases con Francisco. Pero el sueño del niño era muy grande para ser **detenido**, así que él y el músico **seguían** con sus clases a **escondidas**, con ayuda de la abuela quien quería **ayudar** a su nieto a seguir su sueño. Ella amaba mucho escuchar cantar y tocar a Carlos, y solía decir que lo hacía como los **ángeles**.

Una **tarde** Francisco le dice a Carlos, que habrá un festival para cantantes y que el niño debía **participar**, Francisco le daría todo su apoyo. Carlos le **comentó** la **noticia** a su abuela, quien también le **animó** a participar así que Carlos iría al festival.

La tarde antes del festival su papá **descubrió** que el niño seguía con sus clases de música, y **supo** lo del festival, le prohibió ir y le **castigó**. El niño estaba **devastado** al ver que su padre le prohibía hacer lo que más ama, él creía que su sueño había **acabado**, pero su abuela llegó a su **cuarto** y le dijo que irían al festival, que su papá había salido **debido** a que un cliente le llamó y tuvo que ir de **emergencia**. A las afueras de la casa le esperaba Francisco, quien acompañó con la abuela a Carlos al festival.

Cuando el padre llegó a la casa y se encontraba sola, supo a donde se habían ido y fue a **buscar** a Carlos, al llegar al festival el niño estaba **nervioso**, pero Francisco le ayudó a **calmarse** y le dijo que **creyera** en **él mismo** y que estaba muy **orgulloso**. Carlos subió al **escenario** al mismo tiempo que su papá llegó al lugar. El niño comenzó a cantar y el **público** se **estremeció**. Dio todo en el escenario, al terminar todos los **asistentes** los **ovacionaron**. Carlos bajó del escenario feliz, su abuela y Francisco le **felicitaron**. Entonces el niño vio a su papá, él esperaba un **regaño**, pero su padre le **abrazó** fuerte y el niño vio que estaba llorando, le pidió disculpas por no haberlo apoyado antes. Le contó que de pequeño él también tenía un sueño, ser **futbolista**, pero su abuelo le había **obligado** a seguir el negocio familiar, y por eso él creía que Carlos debía seguir la **tradición**, pero al escucharlo en el escenario se **conmovió** y de ahora en adelante le ayudaría a seguir su sueño.

Resumen de la historia

La historia de Carlos nos enseña que hay que luchar por nuestros sueños, él es un niño muy dulce que vive con su papá y su abuela, su sueño es ser un gran artista, pero su papá se opone diciendo que no puede ser músico, que tiene que seguir con el negocio familiar de mecánica. Carlos no quiere renunciar y dejar su gran sueño de lado, conoce a su vecino que es un viejo músico, que le comienza a dar clases de música. Un día llega la oportunidad de que el niño partícipe en un festival, con ayuda de su abuela y del músico; el pequeño logra cantar en el festival, su padre llega al sitio y al escuchar cantar a su hijo cambia de parecer, y comienza a apoyar al niño a cumplir su sueño.

Summary of the story

The story of Carlos teaches us that we must fight for our dreams. He is a sweet boy who lives with his father and grandmother, his goal is to be a great artist, but his father opposes saying that he cannot be a musician. He has to continue with the family business of mechanics. Carlos does not want to give up and leave his great dream aside. He meets his neighbor, an old musician who begins to give him music lessons. One day, comes the opportunity for the little boy to participate in a festival. With help from his grandmother and the musician, the little boy manages to sing at the festival. His father arrives at the site, and upon hearing his son singing changes his mind and begins to support the boy to fulfill his dream.

Vocabulary List

- **Abrazó:** Hug/Embraced.
- **Absurdo:** Absurd/Silly.
- **Acabado:** Finished/Done.
- **Acera:** Sidewalk.
- **Agarró:** Grabbed.
- **Anécdotas:** Anecdotes. (Plural)
- **Ángeles:** Angels. (Plural)
- **Animó:** Encouraged.
- **Aprendió:** Learned.
- **Asistentes:** Assistants. (Plural)
- **Atracción:** Attraction.
- **Ayudar:** Help.
- **Bailaba:** Dance.
- **Bohemio:** Bohemian.
- **Buscar:** Search.
- **Calmarse:** Calm down.
- **Cantaba:** Sang.
- **Cantar:** Sing.
- **Cariño:** Affection.
- **Castigó:** Punished.
- **Comentó:** Commented.
- **Conmovió:** Moved/Trilled.
- **Conocidos:** Known.
- **Conocimientos:** Knowledge. (Plural)
- **Creciera:** Grow.
- **Creyera:** Believe.
- **Cuarto:** Room.
- **Debido:** Due to
- **Descubrió:** Discovered/Find out/ Found.
- **Deseaba:** Wished.
- **Detenido:** Stopped.
- **Devastado:** Devastated.
- **Dueño:** Owner.
- **Él mismo:** Himself.
- **Emergencia:** Emergency.
- **Encendía:** Turned on.
- **Encontrado:** Found/Devised.
- **Enseñarles:** Teach them.
- **Escenario:** Scenario/Stage.
- **Escondidas:** Hidden
- **Estremeció:** Shuddered.
- **Felicitaron:** They congratulated.
- **Futbolista:** Soccer player.
- **Grupo:** Group/Band.
- **Guitarra:** Guitar.
- **Hacerse:** Become.
- **Hijos:** Children.
- **Instrumentos:** Instruments. (Plural)
- **Interés:** Interest.
- **Lamentable:** Regrettable.
- **Lindo:** Nice/Cute.

- **Músico:** Musician.
- **Negocio:** Business.
- **Noticia:** News.
- **Obligado:** Required/Obliged/Force.
- **Orgulloso:** Proud.
- **Ovacionaron:** Cheered/Acclaimed.
- **Participar:** Participate.
- **Pasara:** Spend.
- **Pasatiempo:** Hobby.
- **Pasión:** Passion.
- **Pensando:** Thinking.
- **Piano:** Piano.
- **Populares:** Popular.
- **Prohibió:** Prohibited/Ban/Forbid.
- **Público:** Public/Audience.
- **Regaló:** Gave away.
- **Regaño:** Scolding.
- **Seguían:** Continue/Follow.
- **Sueño:** Dream/Goal.
- **Supo:** Knew.
- **Talento:** Talent.
- **Taller mecánico:** Mechanical workshop.
- **Tarde:** Afternoon/Late.
- **Tocar:** Play/Touch.
- **Tradición:** Tradition.
- **Tranquilo:** Quiet/Calm.
- **Tristemente:** Sadly.
- **Vecino:** Neighbor.
- **Verdadera:** True.
- **Viejo:** Old.
- **Yendo:** Going to.

Questions about the story

1. ¿Cuál era el negocio de la familia de Carlos?

    a. Una panaderia.
    b. Un taller mecanico.
    c. Un restaurant.
    d. Una peluqueria.

2. ¿Cómo se llama el vecino del niño?

    a. Martin.
    b. Pedro.
    c. Jose.
    d. Fransisco.

3. ¿Quién ayuda a Carlos a seguir con sus clases de música?

    a. Su mamá.
    b. Su hermana.
    c. Su abuela.
    d. Su papá.

4. ¿En dónde canta Carlos?

    a. Un local.
    b. Un festival.
    c. Un programa de Televisión.
    d. Ninguna de las anteriores.

5. ¿Con quién vive Carlos?

    a. Con su papá y su abuela.
    b. Con su mamá y su papá.
    c. Con su abuela y tía.
    d. Con su papá y una hermana.

Answers.

1. B - What was Carlos' family business?
2. D - What is the name of the child's neighbor?
3. C - Who helps Carlos to continue with his music lessons?
4. B - Where does Carlos sing?
5. A - With whom does Carlos live?

Chapter Eleven

Basic Vocabulary

Un paseo mexicano/A Mexican Tour

Jessica es una **joven estudiante** de California, **desde** hace mucho tiempo quería **viajar** a México. Le **interesaba** mucho la **cultura**, **tradiciones** y comida de este **país Latinoamericano**. Ella **planeó** todo su viaje queriendo **conocer lugares icónicos** de México, como las **pirámides** que **construyeron** las **antiguas civilizaciones** de los Mayas y los Aztecas, las **playas** hermosas de Cancún y Mazatlán, los **pueblos** tradicionales mexicanos, comidas **típicas**, visitar la **gigantesca** Ciudad de México y ver de cerca las tradiciones del **día de los muertos**.

Al llegar Jessica se encontró con Ana otra joven estudiante mexicana, una **antigua** amiga que conoció en el Internet hace mucho **tiempo atrás**, **quien** sería su **guía** durante su **estadía** en el **país**. Ana llevó primero a Jessica a conocer las ciudades Aztecas y Mayas, llegando a visitar grandes pirámides. Viajaron en **auto, bus, avión** y **tren** por todo México visitando estos sitios arqueológicos. **Cada una** de estas tenían que subir unas **cantidades enormes** de **escaleras** para llegar a las cimas de las pirámides. Donde la **vista** era más que asombrosa. Allí Ana le contó un poco sobre las historias de estas civilizaciones antiguas a Jessica.

Luego de visitar estos lugares hermosos, **regresaron** a la Ciudad de México, la cual es la **ciudad** donde vive Ana. Ella llevó a comer a Jessica los **platos** más típicos de México. La llevó a su **restaurante** favorito, **allí** comieron tacos, mole, y tortas de jamón con **salsa picante**. Jessica nunca había comido comida picante, así que su **reacción** fue muy **graciosa**, las dos **terminaron muertas de risa**.

Las dos **decidieron** pasear por la parte **turística** de la ciudad, donde Jessica **notó** algo muy **singular**. En una **plaza** había **cientos** de personas **reunidas riendo** y **gritando**. Esto **despertó** la **curiosidad** de Jessica y Anna así que se **acercaron** al lugar. Cuando se **aproximaron** Jessica no lo podía **creer**, en medio de la plaza había un **cuadrilátero**. Esa noche se estaba **celebrando** un **evento** de **lucha libre gratuito** para un **acto benéfico**. Nunca en su vida Jessica había visto tal **espectáculo** de **hombres enmascarados** muy coloridos **volando** por los **aires**, **al final** todos estaban muy felices **aplaudiendo** y **donando** dinero para una **organización** que **ayuda** a los **tratamientos** de los niños con cáncer. Las **muchachas** donaron **dinero**, se tomaron **fotos** con los **luchadores**, y se fueron felices por tan **única experiencia**.

Jessica volvió a su hotel para **descansar** y **prepararse** para el día **siguiente**, ya que se **celebraría** el **desfile** de día de muertos. Esta era la **principal** razón por la cual Jessica planeó su viaje para estas **fechas**. Ella quería poder ver con sus **propios ojos** este gran día para los mexicanos y vivir esa experiencia **inigualable**. En el desfile había personas **disfrazadas** de: esqueletos, **parcas** y catrinas infaltables. Jessica estaba **deslumbrada** por los colores, los **atuendos**, y las **maravillas de aquel** desfile.

Ana la llevó a su casa, y al llegar Jessica vio un gran **altar** con **velas**, comida, **objetos** y fotos. Ella le **explicó** a Jessica que en cada casa, y en cada **tumba** del **cementerio** las familias colocaban estos altares, con todo aquello que sus **seres queridos** ya **fallecidos** amaban en vida. Esto se hacía para **honrarlos**, y nunca **olvidarlos**. Ana le **menciona** que en la cultura mexicana este día no es para **llorar**, sino para **festejar**; ya que algunos incluso creían que este podía ser un día en que sus familiares podían visitarlos.

A los dos días, Anna y Jessica se fueron a Cancún, la **última parada** de su viaje. Cuando llegaron Jessica estaba maravillada por aquellas playas **cristalinas**, recorrieron las **costas**, observaron **delfines** y disfrutaron de muchas otras **actividades**. Tres **semanas** pasaron las cuales Jessica conoció lugares, comidas, tradiciones y personas fantásticas. Anna acompañó a Jessica al **aeropuerto**, Jessica le agradeció por ser tan buena **anfitriona**, por mostrarle tantos lugares y tradiciones; por contarle tantas historias y haber compartido con ella. Anna fue una gran amiga, y Jessica le dijo que siempre sería **bienvenida** en su casa. Jessica le respondió que la esperaría en California para mostrarle lugares como ella lo hizo en México, finalmente Jessica se fue feliz por haber hecho su viaje y por todos los **recuerdos** e historias que se llevó a su hogar.

Resumen de la historia

Jessica es una joven estudiante de California que decide viajar a México, donde conoce a Ana, que será su guía en el viaje. Ella la llevará a lugares emblemáticos de México, como las pirámides mayas y aztecas. Es allí donde Ana le cuenta un poco de la historia de estas antiguas culturas a Jessica, la cual estaba muy interesada. A continuación, ella ve y experimenta el Día de los Muertos, una antigua tradición mexicana. Ana explica que en este día en particular, hacen altares y celebran con desfiles. Incluso tuvo la oportunidad de ver la lucha libre mexicana en medio de una plaza. También visitó las hermosas playas que ofrece este país, Jessica vivió un viaje como ningún otro, y siempre lo recordará como uno de sus viajes favoritos.

Summary of the story

Jessica is a young student from California who decides to travel to Mexico, where she meets Ana, who will be her guide on the trip. She will take her to iconic places in Mexico, such as the Mayan and Aztec pyramids. It's there where Ana tells her a bit of the history of these ancient cultures to Jessica, who was very interested. Then she gets to see and experience the Day of the Dead, an ancient Mexican tradition. Ana explains that on this particular day, they make altars and celebrate with parades. She even had the opportunity to see Mexican wrestling in the middle of a square. She also visited the beautiful beaches that this country offers, Jessica lived a trip like no other, and she will always remember it as one of her favorite trips.

Vocabulary List

- **Acercaron:** approached.
- **Actividades:** Activities.
- **Acto benéfico:** Charity event
- **Aeropuerto:** Airport.
- **Aires:** Airs.
- **Al final:** At the end.
- **Al llegar:** Upon arrival.
- **Allí:** There.
- **Altar:** Altar
- **Anfitriona:** Host.
- **Antigua:** Ancient/Old.
- **Aplaudiendo:** Clapping.
- **Aproximaron:** Approximate.
- **Aquel:** That/That one.
- **Atuendos:** Attire.
- **Auto:** Car.
- **Avión:** Plane.
- **Ayuda:** Help.
- **Bienvenida:** Welcome.
- **Bus:** Bus.
- **Cada:** Each
- **Cantidades:** Quantities.
- **Celebrando:** Celebrating.
- **Celebraría:** I would celebrate.
- **Cementerio:** Cemetery.
- **Cientos:** Hundreds.
- **Ciudad:** City.
- **Civilizaciones:** Civilizations.
- **Conocer:** Know.
- **Construyeron:** They built.
- **Costas:** Costs.
- **Creer:** Believe.
- **Cristalinas:** Crystalline.
- **Cuadrilátero:** Ring.
- **Cultura:** Culture.
- **Curiosidad:** Curiosity.
- **Decidieron:** They decided.
- **Delfines:** Dolphins.
- **Descansar:** Rest.
- **Desde:** Since/From.
- **Desfile:** Parade.
- **Deslumbrada:** Dazzled.
- **Despertó:** woke up.
- **Día de los muertos:** Day of the death.
- **Dinero:** Money.
- **Disfrazadas:** Disguised.
- **Donando:** Donating.
- **Enmascarados:** Masked
- **Enormes:** Huge.
- **Escaleras:** Stairs.

- **Espectáculo:** Show.
- **Esqueletos:** Skeletons.
- **Estadía:** Stay.
- **Estudiante:** Student.
- **Evento:** Event.
- **Experiencia:** Experience.
- **Explicó:** explained.
- **Fallecidos:** Deceased.
- **Fechas:** Dates.
- **Festejar:** Celebrate.
- **Fotos:** Photos/Pictures.
- **Gigantesca:** Gigantic.
- **Graciosa:** Funny.
- **Gratuito:** Free.
- **Gritando:** Screaming.
- **Guía:** Guide.
- **Hombres:** Men.
- **Honrarlos:** Honor them.
- **Icónicos:** Iconic.
- **Inigualable:** Unmatched/Unparalleled.
- **Interesaba:** Interested.
- **Joven:** Young.
- **Latinoamericano:** Latin American.
- **Llorar:** Cry.
- **Lucha libre:** Pro-Wrestling.
- **Luchadores:** Fighters/Wrestlers.
- **Lugares:** Places.
- **Maravillas:** Wonders.
- **Menciona:** Mentions.
- **Muchachas:** Girls.
- **Muertas de risa:** Laughing out loud.
- **Notó:** Noted.
- **Objetos:** Objects.
- **Ojos:** Eyes.
- **Olvidarlos:** Forget them.
- **Organización:** Organization.
- **País:** Country.
- **Parada:** Stop.
- **Parcas:** Grim reaper.
- **Pirámides:** Pyramids.
- **Planeó:** Planned.

- **Platos:** Plates.
- **Playas:** Beaches.
- **Plaza:** Square.
- **Prepararse:** Prepare/Getting ready.
- **Principal:** Principal.
- **Propios:** Own.
- **Pueblos:** Villages.
- **Quien:** Who.
- **Reacción:** Reaction.
- **Recuerdos:** Memories/Souvenirs.
- **Regresaron:** They returned.
- **Restaurante:** Restaurant.
- **Reunidas:** Reunited.
- **Riendo:** Laughing.
- **Salsa picante:** Hot sauce.
- **Semanas:** Weeks.
- **Seres queridos:** Loved ones.
- **Siguiente:** Next.
- **Singular:** Unique.
- **Terminaron:** Ended/Finished
- **Tiempo atrás:** Some time ago.
- **Típicas:** Typical/Traditional.
- **Tradiciones:** Traditions.
- **Tratamientos:** Treatments.
- **Tren:** Train.
- **Tumba:** Grave.
- **Turística:** Tourist.
- **Última:** Last.
- **Única:** Only.
- **Velas:** Candles.
- **Viajar:** Travel.
- **Vista:** View.
- **Volando:** Flying.

Questions about the story

1. ¿De dónde era Jessica?

a. San Francisco.
b. Nueva York.
c. Houston.
d. California.

2. ¿Qué vio Jessica en esa plaza en México?

a. Un concierto.
b. Lucha libre.
c. Una obra.
d. A unos payasos.

3. ¿Qué civilizaciones antiguas conoció en el viaje?

a. Azteca y Maya.
b. Inca y Maya.
c. Azteca e Inca.
d. Ninguna de las anteriores.

4. ¿Cómo se llama la guía de Jessica en el viaje?

a. Marta.
b. Ana.
c. Camila.
d. Isis.

5. ¿Qué festejo quería ver en su viaje?

a. El día de los muertos.
b. El día de los vivos.
c. Navidad.
d. Halloween.

Answers

1. **D - Where was Jessica from?**
2. **B - What did Jessica see in that plaza in Mexico?**
3. **A - What ancient civilizations did she meet on the trip?**
4. **B - What is the name of Jessica's guide on the trip?**
5. **A - What celebration did she want to see on her trip?**

Chapter Twelve

Basic Verbs

El universo escucha a Claudia/The Universe Listens to Claudia

Esta historia **comienza** con una mujer que **cree** que el universo la **escucha** y le **responde**. Sus creencias **hacen** que **logre** todo lo que se **proponga**. Todo **empieza** con una niña llamada Claudia, esta carismática joven siempre fue muy optimista, tristemente ella fue una persona con discapacidad, por cosas del destino Claudia **nació** con una enfermedad la cual le **impidió usar** las piernas. Esto nunca fue un problema para ella, ya que siempre se **retaba** desde muy pequeña para **superarse**. Sus padres la **protegían** mucho por su condición, pero Claudia **quería** ser una aventurera, quería **conocer** el mundo, **viajar**, **explorar**, y **logro conseguir** un método para **hacerlo**.

¡Los libros!, en ellos **consiguió** una forma de **escapar**. La lectura le **permitió recorrer** mundos de fantasía, cada vez se **enamoraba** más de los libros, ella **devoró** clásicos como Harry Potter, Señor de los anillos, Canción de Hielo y Fuego, entre otros. Gracias a **leer** estos libros acerca de mundos mágicos, Claudia **desarrollo** una visión del mundo muy única.

A pesar de su discapacidad, siempre **intento vivir** experiencias y nunca **rendirse** a las adversidades, era una chica muy positiva.

Unos años **pasaron** y la pasión de Claudia por los libros **crecía** aún más, **solía analizar** libros de filosofía, psicología, y poesía. Tampoco **podía parar** de leer libros de ciencia ficción, suspenso, y drama, le encanta **actuar** novelas de Shakespeare, solía **inspirarse** mucho al **representar** a Macbeth cuando **actuaba** en su habitación, pero los libros que más le **interesaban** eran los de ciencia y medicina, siempre se estaba **informando** sobre cualquier avance. Lo que más **deseaba** era poder **caminar**, y siempre **pensaba** que lo iba a **lograr**, lo manifestaba al universo, se lo **decía** y hasta lo **gritaba esperando** que el universo **escuchara**.

Claudia creció y se **convirtió** en una mujer de veinte años que **ingreso** a la universidad para **estudiar** Literatura, **eligió** esta carrera porque la adicción a la lectura le **hizo cuestionarse** que quería **hacer** con su vida. **Decidió** que quería **escribir** y **crear** historias, para poder **inspirar** a personas como muchos escritores la inspiraron a ella. Sus días favoritos eran aquellos cuando **iba** a una cafetería cerca de su casa, a **tomar** un café y a estudiar.

Ella creía firmemente en el poder del universo. Le gustaba **manifestar** y **atraer** cosas positivas a su vida. Hubo una época en la que Claudia sé **enfermó** y tenían que **operarla** de emergencia para **salvarle** la vida. Le harían un trasplante de médula ósea, si esta operación era exitosa, no solo **salvaría** su vida, sino también **recuperaría** la sensibilidad en las piernas y podría caminar de nuevo. **Poniendo** en **práctica** todo lo que **aprendió leyendo** sobre fantasía cuando era niña, **empezó** a manifestar, **visualizar** y **decretar** ideas, pensamientos o deseos al universo. La operación fue todo un éxito y ella con mucha fuerza de voluntad se **propuso salir adelante**. No fue fácil, ya que tuvo que **acudir** a terapia física para **recobrar** la movilidad en sus piernas.

Claudia **recordó** que cuando era niña y le manifestó al universo que quería caminar, ahí ella **entendió** que el universo la **escucho**; **logrando** su mayor deseo, poder caminar. Ahora le **queda** otras metas, como **graduarse** y escribir un libro.

Años después logro otro éxito graduándose. Claudia le **agradeció** nuevamente al universo. Tanto era la fe que le tenía en esto que **decidió recoger** información sobre este tema y escribir un libro de ayuda y motivación. Se **basó** en sus propias historia, dificultades y experiencia, para crearlo. Usando el poder de la manifestación como tema principal. Claudia nunca **imaginó** que su libro tendría el éxito que obtuvo. Por muy difícil de creer, termino **vendiendo** miles de copias en todo el mundo.

Su libro se **tradujo** a más de cuatro idiomas, incluso termino **dando** conferencias en grandes auditorios. La primera vez que ella dio una conferencia, se estaba **muriendo** de nervios, le **sudaban** las manos, a pesar de toda las dificultades que había superado en su vida, **hablar** en público era su mayor obstáculo, pero **recordó** como su libro pudo **llegar** a tantas personas para **ayudar** a **mejorar** sus vidas, que no pudo **contener** su felicidad y emoción. Fue en ese momento que ella se **sintió** realizada y agradecida con el universo.

Resumen de la historia

Claudia es una joven muy optimista que cree en el poder del universo, las manifestaciones y los decretos. Nació con una enfermedad que le imposibilitaba el uso de las piernas, pero esto nunca le impidió superarse. Desde pequeña le encantaba leer, y cuando Claudia creció, encontró su pasión en la escritura, eligiendo estudiar literatura. Un día, Claudia cayó enferma y tuvo que ser operada de urgencia. Esta operación le salvó la vida y pudo volver a caminar. Desde que Claudia era una niña, siempre tuve fe en que esto sucedería. Claudia pudo por fin utilizar sus piernas. Tiempo después, decidió contar su experiencia, así que escribió un libro, que acabó teniendo mucho éxito, e incluso dio conferencias.

Summary of the story

Claudia is a very optimistic young woman who believes in the power of the universe, manifestations, and decrees. She was born with a disease that made it impossible for her to use her legs, but this never stopped her from bettering herself. Since she was a little girl, she loved reading, and when Claudia grew up, she found her passion in writing, choosing to study literature. One day, Claudia fell ill and had to undergo emergency surgery. This operation saved her life, and she could walk again. Since Claudia was a little girl, I always had faith that this would happen. Claudia could finally use her legs. Sometime later, she decided to tell her experience, so she wrote a book, which ended up being very successful, and even gave lectures.

<u>Vocabulary list</u>

The majority of the translations and the verbs between the parenthesis are in their infinitive grammatical form. Some Spanish verbs have several meanings. Try to relate them using the context of the story.

- **Actuar:** Act.
- **Acudir:** Go to.
- **Agradeció (Agradecer):** Thank/Appreciate.
- **Analizar:** Analyze.
- **Aprendió (Aprender):** Learn.
- **Atraer:** Attract.
- **Ayudar:** Help.
- **Basó (Basar):** Base.
- **Caminar:** Walk.
- **Comienza:** Start.
- **Conocer:** Know/Meet/Visit.
- **Conseguir:** Get/Achieve.
- **Convirtió (Convertir):** Convert/Change.

- **Crear:** Create/Build.
- **Crecía (Crecer):** Grow.
- **Cree (Creer):** Believe.
- **Cuestionarse (Cuestionar):** Question.
- **Dando (Dar):** Give.
- **Decía (Decir):** Say.
- **Decidió (Decidir):** Decide.
- **Decretar:** Decree.
- **Desarrollo (Desarrollar):** Develop/Evolve.
- **Deseaba (Desear):** Wish.
- **Devoró (Devorar):** Devour.
- **Eligió (Elegir):** Choose.
- **Empezó (Empezar):** Start/Begin.
- **Enamoraba (Enamorar):** To fall in love.
- **Enfermó (Enfermar):** Sick.
- **Entendió (Entender):** Understand.
- **Escapar:** Escape.
- **Escribir:** Write.
- **Escuchará (Escuchar):** Listen.
- **Esperando (Esperar):** Wait.
- **Estudiar:** Study.
- **Explorar:** Explore.
- **Fue (Es/Ir):** Be/Go.
- **Graduarse (Graduar):** Graduate.
- **Gritaba (Gritar):** Scream.
- **Hablar:** Speak/Talk.
- **Hacer:** Make/Do.
- **Hizo (Hacer):** Make/Do
- **Iba (Ir):** Go.
- **Imaginó (Imaginar):** Imagine.
- **Impidió (Impedir):** Prevent.
- **Informando (Informar):** Inform.
- **Ingreso (Ingresar):** Enter.
- **Inspirar:** Inspire.
- **Inspirarse (Inspirar):** Inspire.
- **Intento (Intentar):** Try.
- **Interesaban (Interesar):** Interest.
- **Leer:** Read.
- **Leyendo (Leer):** Read.
- **Llegar:** Reach/Arrive/Get.
- **Logrando (Lograr):** Achieve.

- **Lograr:** Achieve.
- **Logre (Lograr):** Achieve.
- **Logro (Lograr):** Achieve.
- **Manifestar:** Manifest.
- **Mejorar:** Improve.
- **Muriendo (Morir):** Die.
- **Nació (Nacer):** Born.
- **Operarla (Operar):** Operate.
- **Parar:** Stop
- **Pasaron (Pasar):** Pass.
- **Pensaba (Pensar):** Think.
- **Permitió (Permitir):** Allow.
- **Podía (Poder):** Can/Able to.
- **Poniendo (Poner):** Put.
- **Práctica (Practicar):** Practice.
- **Proponga (Proponer):** Propose.
- **Propuso (Proponer):** Propose.
- **Protegían (Proteger):** Protect
- **Queda (Quedar):** Remain.
- **Quería (Querer):** Remain.
- **Recobrar:** Recover.
- **Recoger:** Collet/Pick.
- **Recordó (Recordar):** Remember/Recall/Remind.
- **Recorrer:** Visit.
- **Recuperaría (Recuperar):** Retrieve.
- **Rendirse (Rendir):** Rendir.
- **Representar:** Represent
- **Responde (Responder):** Reply.
- **Retaba (Retar):** Challenge.
- **Salir adelante:** Get ahead.
- **Salvaría (Salvar):** Save.
- **Solía (Soler):** Use to.
- **Sudaban (Sudar):** Sweat.
- **Superarse (Superar):** Overcome.
- **Tomar:** Take.
- **Tradujo (Traducir):** Translate.
- **Usar:** Use.
- **Vendiendo (Vender):** Sell
- **Viajar:** Travel.
- **Visualizar:** View
- **Vivir:** Live.

Questions about the story

1. ¿Cuál carrera decidió estudiar Claudia?

    a. Matemáticas.

    b. Ingeniería.

    c. Literatura.

    d. Arquitectura.

2. ¿Qué cirugía realizaron en Claudia?

    a. Trasplante de médula ósea.

    b. Trasplante de corazón.

    c. Trasplante de pierna.

    d. Ninguna de las anteriores.

3. ¿Cuál libro Claudia solía actuar?

    a. Romeo y Julieta.

    b. Macbeth.

    c. Señor de los Anillos

    d. Harry Potter.

4. ¿Cuántos idiomas tradujeron el libro de Claudia?

    a. Tres.

    b. Dos.

    c. Cinco.

    d. Ninguna de las anteriores.

5. ¿En qué creía Claudia?

    a. En el universo.

    b. En los planetas.

    c. En los animales.

    d. En nada.

Answers

1. C - What career did Claudia decide to study?
2. A - What surgery did you perform on Claudia?
3. B - Which book did Claudia use to act?
4. D - How many languages has Claudia's book been translated into?
5. A - What did Claudia believe in?

Chapter Thirteen

Basic Adjectives

Un viaje a Río/A Trip to Rio

Hola, mi nombre es Juan, tengo doce años, y les contaré mi experiencia **increíble** en el **famoso** desfile de Río de Janeiro en Brasil. Soy un niño **tranquilo**, **amable**, **inteligente** y muy **observador**. Mi cabello es de color **marrón castaño**, mis ojos son **negros** como los de mi padre. Un músico **talentoso, alto, calvo, algo callado** y **cariñoso**. Un día recibió una invitación **inesperada** para tocar con una orquesta en el festival de Río, específicamente en el desfile.

Mi papá recibió esta invitación porque es un músico **virtuoso reconocido**. Él suele tocar en estadios y teatros con cientos de personas escuchando sus canciones. Los instrumentos que él suele tocar son: el saxofón, este es un instrumento **curvo**, algo **pesado, duro, metálico,** y de color **dorado**; el violín, este es un instrumento **liviano, pequeño, delicado, sólido**; el piano, el cual es un instrumento **enorme**, muy pesado, **complejo,** y **elegante**; su instrumento favorito, la guitarra, la cual es **mediana**, algo **liviana, hermosa, hueca, melodiosa** y **rítmica**.

Mi papá recibió esa invitación en un día **soleado**, mientras estábamos en el mercado comprando verduras, estas estaban **frescas** y **sabrosas**. Al leer el correo electrónico quedó **sorprendido**, algo **angustiado** pero **emocionado**. Cuando llego a casa lo consulto con mi mamá, ella le dijo que lo aceptara de **inmediato**. Mi papá respondió la invitación y nos preparamos para este **gran** y largo viaje a Brasil. Este viaje fue muy **difícil** y **accidentado**, porque tuvimos muchos contratiempos, perdimos nuestro equipaje y nuestro vuelo por el clima, con vientos **turbulentos** y truenos **poderosos**. Al final aterrizamos de manera **segura**, y como dije anteriormente nuestro equipaje se perdió, estuvimos en el aeropuerto esperando nuestro equipaje. Las maletas de mis padres eran **cuadradas, rectangulares,** de color **vino tinto, azul claro, verde oscuro,** y la mía era **redonda** y **multicolor**, vimos **numerosas** maletas de muchas formas, incluso vimos maletas **triangulares**, pero al final aparecieron.

Perdimos mucho tiempo en el aeropuerto, pero al final nos dirigimos al hotel, en el camino recorrimos una **pequeña** parte de Río de Janeiro. Primero visitamos una playa, podía sentir la arena **caliente** debajo de mis pies, el viento soplaba **fuerte**, el agua era **refrescante**. Luego pasamos por calles **concurridas** y por lugares **pintorescos**, fue **asombroso**.

Llegó el gran día, y yo estaba **entusiasmado** sentado en las gradas algo **hambriento**, le pedí a mi madre que me comprara golosinas, ella me compro muchas, algunas eran **ácidas**, otras **amargas**, pero la mayoría eran **dulces**, también me compró una hamburguesa, pero no olía muy bien era **asquerosa**.

Estaba bastante **aburrido** porque no pasaba nada, hasta que de repente hubo fuegos artificiales, el desfile comenzó y todo fue **mágico**, había mujeres **guapas** y muy **elegantes** bailando de manera **ordenada** como en una coreografía mientras las carrozas pasan, esta primera carroza era **gigantesca**, con **múltiples** colores, algo **extravagante** era como un dinosaurio algo **aterrador**. La siguiente carroza era más pequeña, pero bastante **ancha**, los colores eran más **opacos**, pero en general la carroza era muy **divertida**, eran unos gatos **gordos** de color **naranja**, parecido a Garfield.

La siguiente carroza estaba **llena** de músicos de samba, era toda una fiesta, toda la gente brincaba y se movía de manera **desordenada** en las gradas, era una locura. Hubo un sin fin de carrozas, algunas eran muy **inocentes**, otras muy **atrevidas**, eso sí todas tenían muchas cosas en común, como ser **ruidosas**, **coloridas** y **extravagantes**; no hubo ninguna que fuera **modesta**.

Finalmente, mi papá aparece en una carroza **monstruosa** que lanzaba fuegos artificiales y confeti. Empecé a llorar **orgulloso** por ver a mi papá tocar **apasionado**, siempre se le vio **determinado** de dar un buen espectáculo. Mi papá deleitó a los cientos de espectadores y a los millones que veían el desfile por televisión. No puedo explicar lo que se sintió ver a las personas presentes levantarse de sus asientos y empezar a aplaudir a la gran orquesta en la cual estaba tocando mi papá, a pesar de que estaba bastante **alejado** de él, yo podía ver que le bajaban lágrimas de **alegría**, y eso me hizo el joven más **feliz** de Brasil y tal vez del mundo.

Resumen de la historia

Esta breve historia cuenta el viaje de Juan y su familia a Río de Janeiro. Su padre es un gran músico que es invitado a tocar en el desfile de Río. Sin pensarlo dos veces, el padre acepta y se lleva a toda la familia a unas cortas vacaciones. Aunque hay varios contratiempos, la familia consigue llegar a Brasil. Van a varios lugares de la ciudad. Pero lo más importante es ver el desfile. Juan y su madre se sientan a ver muchas carrozas bonitas y coloridas hasta que ven al padre, lo que hace que el momento sea muy emotivo.

Summary of the story

This short story tells the story of Juan and his family's trip to Rio de Janeiro. His father is a great musician who is invited to play in Rio's parade. Without thinking twice, the father accepts, taking the whole family on a short vacation. Although there are several setbacks, the family manages to get to Brazil. They go to several places in the city. But the most important thing is to see the parade. Juan and his mother sit and watch many beautiful and colorful floats until they watch the father, which makes the moment very emotional.

Vocabulary List

- **Aburrido:** Boring.
- **Accidentado:** Rough/Uneven.
- **Ácidas:** Acids/Sour.
- **Alegría:** Joy.
- **Alejado:** Away.
- **Alto:** Tall.
- **Amable:** Kind/Friendly.
- **Amargas:** Bitter.
- **Ancha (o):** Wide.
- **Angustiado:** Anguished.
- **Apasionado:** Passionate.
- **Asombroso:** Amazing.
- **Asquerosa:** Grows.
- **Aterrador:** Terrifying.
- **Atrevidas:** Bold/Daring.
- **Azul claro:** Light blue.
- **Caliente:** Hot.
- **Calvo:** Bald.
- **Callado:** Silent.
- **Cariñoso:** Affectionate/Loving.
- **Coloridas:** Colorful.
- **Complejo:** Complex.
- **Concurridas:** Concurred.
- **Cuadradas:** Squares.
- **Curvo:** Curved.
- **Delicado:** Delicate.
- **Desordenada:** Messy.
- **Determinado:** Determined.
- **Difícil:** Difficult.
- **Divertida:** Fun.
- **Dorado:** Gold.
- **Dulce:** Sweet.
- **Duro:** Hard.
- **Elegante:** Elegant.
- **Emocionado:** Excited.
- **Enorme:** Huge.
- **Entusiasmado:** Enthusiastic.
- **Extravagante:** Extravagant.
- **Famoso:** Famous.
- **Feliz:** Happy
- **Frescas:** Fresh.
- **Fuerte:** Strong.
- **Gigantesca:** Gigantic.
- **Gordos:** Fat.
- **Gran:** Great.
- **Guapas:** Pretty.
- **Hambriento:** Hungry.
- **Hermosa:** Beautiful.
- **Hueca:** Hollow.
- **Increíble:** Incredible.
- **Inesperada:** Unexpected.
- **Inmediato:** Immediate.
- **Inocentes:** Innocents.
- **Inteligente:** Smart.
- **Liviana (o):** Light.
- **Llena:** Full.

- **Mágico:** Magic.
- **Marrón castaño:** Chestnut brown.
- **Mediana:** Median/Middle/Avarage.
- **Melodiosa:** Melodious.
- **Metálico:** Metalic.
- **Modesta:** Modest.
- **Monstruosa:** Monstrous.
- **Multicolor:** Multicolor.
- **Múltiples:** Multiple.
- **Naranja:** Orange.
- **Negros:** Black.
- **Numerosas:** Numerous.
- **Observador:** Observer.
- **Opacos:** Opaque.
- **Ordenada:** Orderly/Tidy.
- **Orgulloso:** Proud.
- **Pequeña (o):** Small/Little.
- **Pesado:** Heavy.
- **Pintorescos:** Picturesque.
- **Poderosos:** Powerful.
- **Reconocido:** Recognized.
- **Rectangulares:** Rectangulares.
- **Redonda:** Round.
- **Refrescante:** Refreshing.
- **Rítmica:** Rhythmic.
- **Ruidosas:** Noisy.
- **Sabrosas:** Tasty.
- **Segura:** Safe.
- **Soleado:** Sunny.
- **Sólido:** Solid.
- **Sorprendido:** Surprised.
- **Talentoso:** Talented.
- **Tranquilo:** Quiet/Calm.
- **Triangulares:** Triangular.
- **Turbulentos:** Turbulent.
- **Verde oscuro:** Dark green.
- **Vino Tinto:** Red wine.
- **Virtuoso:** Virtuous.

Questions about the story

1. ¿Dónde estaba el padre de Juan cuando recibió la invitación?

    a. En el Mercado.

    b. En la casa.

    c. En el parque.

    d. Ninguna de las anteriores.

2. ¿Por qué no se comió la hamburguesa Juan?

    a. Sabia horrible.

    b. Olía Asqueroso.

    c. Porque tenía lechuga.

    d. Porque no tenía hambre.

3. ¿Qué tenía la segunda carroza que la hacía lucir divertida?

    a. Gatos gordos.

    b. Gatos flacos.

    c. Perros gordos.

    d. Dinosaurios.

4. ¿Cuál es la forma de la maleta de Juan?

    a. Triangular.

    b. Rectangular.

    c. Cuadrada.

    d. Circular.

5. ¿Cuál es el instrumento que es hueco?

    a. El piano.

    b. La batería.

    c. La guitarra.

    d. Ninguna de las anteriores.

Answers

    1. A - Where was Juan's father when he received the invitation?

    2. B - Why didn't Juan eat the hamburger?

    3. A - What was it about the second float that made it look fun?

    4. D - What is the shape of Juan's suitcase?

    5. C - Which instrument is hollow?

Chapter Fourteen

Basic Vocabulary

Clases de manejo/Driving Lessons

Hola, mi nombre es Alejandra, y **hoy** tengo mi primera **clase** de **manejo**. Me siento un poco nerviosa, pero estoy **lista**. Yo nunca he **manejado**, ya que siempre mis padres, mi hermano o mi **novio** me llevan a cualquier lugar al que tengo que ir, o **por lo general** tomo el **transporte público**, como **autobuses**, taxis, Uber, **metro**, etc.

Estoy **cansada** de **depender** de **los demás**, es hora de **crecer** un poco y ser **independiente**. El primer paso es **aprender** a **conducir**, ya que nadie tiene tiempo para **enseñarme, me dirigí** a la **escuela de manejo**, en la **zona sur** de la ciudad. En camino paso por una **venta** de autos, aunque muchos son **usados** se ven en muy buen **estado**, ahí veo un auto **compacto** pequeño de color **gris**, me quedo mirando a este coche, **imaginándome** un **sin fin** de **situaciones** donde, **conduzco** este lindo auto, además no es **tan caro** así que me **pondré** una meta, trabajaré duro este año para poder comprarlo.

Al llegar a la escuela de manejo me dicen quién va a ser mi **instructor**, su nombre es Juan es muy **amable** y **cordial**. Lo primero que hace es llevarme a un **salón** para **explicarme** lo **básico**, como por **ejemplo**, cómo **funciona** el auto y sus **partes**, como las **ruedas, volante, motor**, etc. También me enseño las **reglas de seguridad**, y las **señales** de **tránsito**. Luego nos **dirigimos** al auto, mientras entramos me enseña cómo ponerme el **cinturón** de seguridad, me indica algunas **medidas** de **precaución**, y me enseña a **encender** el **vehículo**, como jugar con los **pedales**, y en especial la **técnica** con el **embrague**. Al terminar de explicarme lo básico, me pide que encienda el **vehículo** y realicé todos los pasos que me acabo de enseñar.

Primero miró que los **espejos retrovisores** estén **ubicados** perfectamente, luego me pongo el cinturón de **seguridad, verificó** que la **caja de velocidades** esté en **neutro, posteriormente** enciendo el vehículo, remuevo el **freno de mano**, pisó el **freno** y el embrague, verifico que es seguro para salir, suelto el freno, y poco a poco voy soltando el embrague mientras **piso** el **acelerador** lentamente. La primera vez que intente esto se me **apagó** el auto, la segunda vez el auto salió **disparado bruscamente** me llene de nervios y frene de golpe, pero en mi tercer intento lo pude hacer, como dice el dicho **la tercera es la vencida.**

Llegó el momento de tomar algunas curvas, estaba bastante nerviosa y mientras lo hago, el instructor **me gritó** fuerte, porque me estaba **acercando** a una **pared** muy **peligrosamente**, rápidamente yo frene llena de nervios. El instructor se **disculpó** y me dice que no debo tomar las curvas tan **cerradas**, luego me dice que hagamos otro **intento**, vuelvo hacer el **mismo procedimiento** tomando mejor las curvas y esta vez me sale mucho mejor, el instructor me va explicando cómo ir jugando con el acelerador, me dice que **escuche** el **motor** o mire las **revoluciones** en el **tablero**, esto me va a indicar como acelerar y cuándo hacer los cambios de velocidad. Luego de 2 horas ya sabía lo básico y podría dar algunas vueltas por la **pista** de la escuela. Así terminó mi primer día en la escuela de manejo ya estoy esperando con **emoción** mis siguientes clases.

Al llegar a casa, mi padre me pregunta cómo estuvo mi primera clase, yo le digo que me fue muy bien y le explico todo lo que aprendí. Como **recompensa** me invita a **cenar**, y me deja conducir su auto, aunque eso es algo **irresponsable**, ya que apenas estoy aprendiendo, pero igual lo hice, en el camino mi padre me **orientaba** y me daba más **consejos**, me dirigí a la **zona norte** de la ciudad donde comimos **helado** y pizza. Después de un día bastante **productivo** me siento **satisfecha** y orgullosa de **mí misma**; ahora estoy llena de **motivación** para trabajar **arduamente** y poder comprarme mi **propio** auto. Aunque el viaje es largo sé que lo lograré.

Resumen de la historia

Alejandra es una joven con muchas ganas de empezar a independizarse, ella está cansada de que su padre, su hermano o su novio la lleven a todos lados. Como nadie le quiere enseñar a manejar, ella decide ir por sus propios medios a una escuela de manejo. Allí conoce a Juan su instructor, que le enseña todos los principios básicos para empezar a manejar. Después de una larga clase ella regresa a su casa feliz porque aprendió lo esencial. Ella quiere tener su propio auto, y le gustaría comprar un pequeño compacto que vio antes de ir a la clase de manejo. Su padre la felicita por haber aprendido y como recompensa la lleva a cenar, en camino le da lecciones extra. Después de compartir una linda cena con su padre, sigue pensando en que quiere ser independiente y trabajar duro para lograrlo.

Summary of the story

Alejandra is a young woman eager to become independent. She is tired of being driven everywhere by her father, her brother, or her boyfriend. Since no one wants to teach her how to drive, she decides to go to a driving school on her own. There Alejandra meets Juan, her instructor, who teaches her all the basics to start driving. After a long class, she returns home happy because she learned the basics. She wants to have her own car and would like to buy a small compact she saw before going to the driving class. Her father congratulates her for learning and takes her out to dinner as a reward, giving her extra lessons on the way. After sharing a nice dinner with her father, she keeps thinking that she wants to be independent and work hard to achieve it.

Vocabulary List

- **Acelerador:** Accelerator.
- **Acercando:** Approaching.
- **Amable:** kind.
- **Apagó:** Turned off.
- **Aprender:** Learn.
- **Arduamente:** Arduously.
- **Autobuses:** Bus.
- **Básico:** Basic.
- **Bruscamente:** Abruptly
- **Caja de velocidades:** Gearbox/Transmission.
- **Cansada:** Tired.
- **Caro:** Expensive.
- **Cenar:** Dinner.
- **Cerradas:** Closed.
- **Cinturón:** Belt/Seatbelt.
- **Clase:** Class.
- **Compacto:** Compact.
- **Conducir:** Drive.
- **Conduzco:** I drive.
- **Consejos:** Tips/Advices.
- **Cordial:** Friendly/Cordial.
- **Crecer:** Grow/Expand.
- **Depender:** Rely on/Rely upon.
- **Dirigimos:** We headed.
- **Disculpó:** Apologized.
- **Disparado:** Shot.
- **Ejemplo:** Example.
- **Embrague:** Clutch.
- **Emoción:** Excitement/Emotion.
- **Encender:** Turn on/Ignite/Start.
- **Enseñarme:** Teach me.
- **Escuche:** Listen to.
- **Escuela de manejo:** Driving school.
- **Espejos retrovisores:** Rearview mirrors.
- **Estado:**State/Status/Condition.
- **Explicarme:** Explain to me.
- **Freno:** Brake.
- **Freno de mano:** Hand brake.
- **Funciona:** Work/Funtion/Operate.
- **Gris:** Grey.
- **Helado:** Ice Cream.
- **Hoy**: Today.
- **Imaginándome:** Imagining me.
- **Independiente:** Independent.
- **Instructor:** Teacher/Instructor.
- **Intento:** Attempt.
- **La tercera es la vencida:** Third time's the charm.

- **Lista:** Ready.
- **Los demás:** Everybody else/The other.
- **Manejado:** Driven/Managed.
- **Manejo:** Drive/Management.
- **Me dirigí:** I headed.
- **Me gritó:** shouted at me.
- **Medidas:** Measures.
- **Metro:** Subway.
- **Mí misma:** Myself.
- **Mismo:** Same.
- **Motivación:** Motivation.
- **Motor:** Engine.
- **Neutro:** Neutral.
- **Novio:** Boyfriend.
- **Orientaba:** Oriented/Guide.
- **Pared:** Wall.
- **Partes:** Parts.
- **Pedales:** Pedals.
- **Peligrosamente:** Dangerously.
- **Piso:** Floor.
- **Pista:** Track.
- **Pondré:** I will put.
- **Por lo general:** Generally/Usually.
- **Posteriormente:** Subsequently.
- **Precaución:** Caution.
- **Procedimiento:** Procedure.
- **Productivo:** Productive.
- **Propio:** Own.
- **Recompensa:** Reward.
- **Reglas:** Rules.
- **Revoluciones:** Revolutions.
- **Ruedas:** Wheels.
- **Salón:** Room/Hall.
- **Satisfecha:** Satisfied/Pleased.
- **Seguridad:** Security.
- **Señales:** Signals/Sings
- **Sin fin:** Endless.
- **Situaciones:** Situations.
- **Tablero:** Board.
- **Tan:** Such/That.
- **Técnica:** Technique.
- **Tránsito:** Transit.
- **Transporte público:** Public transportation.
- **Ubicados:** Located.
- **Usados:** Used.
- **Vehículo:** Vehicle.
- **Venta:** Sale.
- **Verificó:** Verified.
- **Volante:** Steering wheel.
- **Zona norte:** North zone.
- **Zona sur:** South zone.

Questions about the story

1. **¿Por qué Alejandra quiere aprender a conducir?**

    a. Por gusto.
    b. Por ser independiente.
    c. Por ser dependiente.
    d. Todas las anteriores.

2. **¿Cuál es el color del auto que Alejandra quiere comprar?**

    a. Azul.
    b. Negro.
    c. Rojo.
    d. Gris.

3. **¿Qué paso cuando Alejandra decidió acelerar el auto por primera vez?**

    a. Se apagó.
    b. Se encendió.
    c. No paso nada.
    d. Salio disparada.

4. **¿Por qué le grito el instructor a Alejandra?**

    a. Por acercarse a una pared.
    b. Por alejarse de una pared.
    c. Por frenar.
    d. Ninguna de las anteriores.

5. **¿Quién le compro la pizza a Alejandra al final de la historia?**

    a. Su novio.
    b. Su hermano.
    c. Su instructor.
    d. Su papá.

Answers

1. B - Why does Alejandra want to learn to drive?
2. D - What is the color of the car Alejandra wants to buy?
3. A - What happened when Alejandra decided to accelerate the car for the first time?
4. A - Why did the instructor yell at Alejandra?
5. D - Who bought Alejandra's pizza at the end of the story?

Chapter Fifteen

Basic Vocabulary

El secreto del universo/The Secret of the Universe.

Hace muchos años **existió** un lugar **impresionante** con una **civilización** muy **avanzada**, con **tecnología** tan avanzada que nuestras **humildes mentes** se les hace **imposible comprender**. Este **sitio** se llamaba la Ciudad **Marfil**, en un **planeta** llamado Thessio, ubicado en una **galaxia** no muy **lejana** a la nuestra a **treinta mil años luz**. Los **habitantes** de este mundo eran **parecidos** a **nosotros**, tenían dos **pies**, dos **piernas**, dos **brazos**, dos **manos** con diez **dedos**, un **pecho**, una **cintura**; una **cabeza** con forma **puntiaguda** y **tentáculos** pequeños en el **tope**, con una **boca**, con una **nariz**, una **boca**, dos **orejas**, y dos **ojos**, su color de piel era azul. Sus conocimientos eran muy **vastos**, lograron **entender** cómo funcionaba el **universo**, lograron obtener **energía limpia** e **infinita** de las estrellas, lograron **desarrollar** un **armamento** extremadamente **poderoso**, pero esta raza llamada los asarianos era un pueblo muy **sabio** de naturaleza **pacífica**, su filosofía era la **paz**.

La ciudad era muy bella y tranquila, estaba rodeada de árboles **violetas**, un cielo rojo, y en especial un **mar** vasto, ya que esta ciudad era una gran **isla**. Contaba con calles largas muy **futuristas**, con una estructura muy **avanzada** en sus edificios, su **arquitectura** e **ingeniería** eran únicas. La ciudad vivía en total **armonía**, no existía la **discriminación**, la **violencia**, la **delincuencia**, ni la **maldad**. La ciudad estaba **protegida** por un gran **escudo transparente** el cual **cubría** toda la ciudad. Era un lugar donde la vida era muy **apreciada**, no solo la asariana sino también la animal y **vegetal**. Era un pueblo con grandes **conocimientos matemáticos** y **físicos**, **químicos**, **astronómicos** y **cuánticos** eran **asombrosos**. Lograron **descubrir** cómo se creó el **universo**, cuál es su **propósito** y que hay **más allá**, este gran **secreto** era **resguardado** en el **corazón** de la ciudad llamado la ciudadela, un castillo **indestructible** de **máxima seguridad**.

A pesar de que la vida en ciudad Marfil era tranquila y **armoniosa**. Tenían un **enemigo**, unos temibles seres de aspecto **tenebroso**, de **piel gris**, varios ojos, con **cuernos**, **parecidos** a **insectos** llamados los **espectros**. Estos seres querían **adueñarse** de la ciudad Marfil, no solo obtener su **armamento**, sino también el gran secreto del universo.

Hace muchos años, los antiguos **habitantes** de Ciudad Marfil **lucharon en contra** de los espectros, y los **derrotaron** debido a que los asaríamos tenían las mejores **armas** de la galaxia. Los espectros se **retiraron derrotados, desaparecieron** por un largo tiempo. Pasaron **siglos** desde ese último ataque, pero todo cambió en un día normal como cualquier otro, todo estaba muy tranquilo en la ciudad. Los asarianos estaban haciendo sus **respectivas actividades**, los niños jugaban y todo parecía ir bien, pero de un momento a otro comenzaron a **caer** sobre el escudo cientos de naves de guerra, estas naves disparaban una **sustancia** que **debilita** el **escudo** que **protege** a la ciudad, además había otras naves que disparan rayos láser, **los cuales impactan** y hacían daño en el escudo

Los habitantes comenzaron a correr **asustados** por el **sorpresivo** ataque, y rápidamente los **soldados desplegaron** el **protocolo** de **defensa** de la ciudad. Empezaron a **contraatacar** con todas sus **fuerzas**, con sus **naves**, y **sus** armas **antiaéreas**. Comenzaron a disparar a los invasores, ahí es cuando **se dan cuenta** de que el ejército enemigo eran los espectros **quienes** volvían mucho más armados y avanzados que la última vez.

Han pasado días de **combate**, la ciudad **sufrió** muchos **daños**, el escudo está muy **debilitado**. Los soldados y habitantes se encontraban **entre la espada y la pared**, el escudo comienza a **fallar**. **Si** los espectros logran **entrar**, **mataran** a todos los habitantes, se **adueñarán** del armamento y lo más importante, el secreto del universo. Los asarianos saben que si los espectros **obtienen** estos conocimientos serán una amenaza para las demás civilizaciones en el universo. Así que los asarianos **tomaron** la decisión más radical que les **quedaba**, que era **hundir** la ciudad con todos **ellos**.

El secreto del universo es muy poderoso, y en manos **equivocadas** puede causar mucho daño, **dolor** y **sufrimiento**. Así que los asarianos **sacrifican** sus vidas para salvar al resto de civilizaciones por un **bien mayor**.

Resumen de la historia

La historia de los asarianos comenzó en una galaxia no muy lejana a la nuestra. Esta civilización era muy avanzada, con una mentalidad y filosofía pacífica. Hicieron muchos descubrimientos en física, física cuántica, química, astronomía, matemáticas, etc. Tenían el armamento más avanzado de toda la galaxia a pesar de su forma de vida pacífica. Consiguen obtener energía limpia de las estrellas. Su mayor logro fue el descubrimiento del secreto del universo. Los asarianos descubrieron cómo se creó el universo y cuál es su propósito.

Los espectros eran una civilización malvada que quería este conocimiento para conquistar todo el universo. Atacaron a los asarianos por sorpresa, y lucharon durante muchos días cuando los asarianos fueron derrotados. En un intento de proteger el secreto del universo, decidieron hundir su capital, la Ciudad de Marfil en el oceano, ya que esta quedaba en una isla en medio de un gran mar, para proteger a las demás civilizaciones del universo. Por un bien mayor.

Summary of the story

The story of the Asarians began in a galaxy not so far away from ours. This civilization was ultra-advanced, with a pacific mindset and philosophy. They made many discoveries in physics, quantum physics, chemistry, astronomy, maths, etc. They had the most advanced weaponry in the whole galaxy even though their pacific way of life. They achieve to get clean energy from the stars. Their greatest achievement was the discovery of the secret of the universe. The Asarians discovered how the universe was created and what it is his purpose.

The specters were an evil civilization that wanted this knowledge to conquer the entire universe. They attacked the Asarians by surprise, and They battled for many days when the Asarians were defeated. In an attempt to protect the secret of the universe, they decided to sink their capital, the Ivory City in the ocean, since it was located on an island in the middle of a great sea, in order to protect the other civilizations of the universe. For the greater good.

Vocabulary List

- **Actividades:** Activities.
- **Adueñarán:** They will take over.
- **Adueñarse:** To take over.
- **Antiaéreas:** Anti-aircraft.
- **Años:** Years.
- **Apreciada:** Appreciate/Value/Prized.
- **Armamento:** Armament/Weaponry.
- **Armas:** Weapons.
- **Armonía:** Harmony.
- **Armoniosa:** Harmonious.
- **Arquitectura:** Architecture.
- **Asombrosos:** Amazing.
- **Astronómicos:** Astronomical.
- **Asustados:** Scared/Frightened.
- **Avanzada:** Advanced.
- **Bien mayor:** Greater good.
- **Boca:** Mouth.
- **Brazos:** Arms.
- **Cabeza:** Head.
- **Caer:** Falling.
- **Cintura:** Waist.
- **Civilización:** Civilization.
- **Combate:** Combat.
- **Comprender:** Understand.
- **Conocimientos:** Knowledge.
- **Contraatacar:** Fight back/ Counterattack.
- **Corazón:** Heart.
- **Cuántico:** Quantum.
- **Cubría:** Covers.
- **Cuernos:** Horns.
- **Daños:** Damages.
- **Debilita:** Weaken.
- **Debilitado:** Weakened.
- **Dedos:** Fingers.
- **Defensa:** Defense.
- **Delincuencia:** Delinquency.
- **Derrotados:** Defeated.
- **Desaparecieron:** Disappeared.
- **Desarrollar:** Develop.
- **Descubrir:** Discover.
- **Desplegaron:** They deployed.
- **Discriminación:** Discrimination.
- **Dolor:** Pain.
- **Ellos:** They.
- **En contra:** Against.
- **Enemigo:** Enemy.
- **Energía:** Energy.
- **Entender:** Understand/Get.
- **Entrar:** Enter.
- **Entre la espada y la pared:** Between a rock and a hard place.
- **Equivocadas:** Wrong.
- **Escudo:** Shield.
- **Existió:** Existed.
- **Fallar:** Fail.
- **Físicos:** Physical.
- **Fuerzas:** Forces.
- **Futuristas:** Futurists.
- **Galaxia:** Galaxy.
- **Gris:** Grey.
- **Habitantes:** Inhabitants.
- **Humildes:** Humble.
- **Hundir:** Sink.
- **Impactan:** Impact.
- **Imposible:** Impossible.
- **Impresionante:** Impressive.
- **Indestructible:** Indestructible.
- **Infinita:** Infinite.
- **Ingeniería:** Engineering.
- **Insectos:** Insects.
- **Isla:** Island.
- **Lejana:** Far.
- **Limpia:** Clean.
- **Los cuales:** Which.
- **Lucharon:** They fought.

- **Luz:** Light.
- **Maldad:** Evil.
- **Manos:** Hands.
- **Mar:** Sea.
- **Marfil:** Evory.
- **Más allá:** Beyond.
- **Matarán:** They will kill.
- **Matemáticos:** Mathematical.
- **Máxima:** Maximum.
- **Mentes:** Minds.
- **Nariz:** Nose.
- **Naves:** Ships/Spaceships.
- **Nosotros:** We.
- **Obtienen:** Obtain.
- **Ojos:** Eyes.
- **Orejas:** Ears.
- **Pacífica:** Peaceful.
- **Parecidos:** Similarities.
- **Paz:** Peace.
- **Pecho:** Chest.
- **Piel:** Skin.
- **Piernas:** Legs.
- **Pies:** Feet.
- **Planeta:** Planet.
- **Poderoso:** Powerful.
- **Propósito:** Purpose.
- **Protege:** Protect.
- **Protegida:** Protected.
- **Protocolo:** Protocol.
- **Puntiaguda:** Pointed.
- **Quedaba:** To be left/Remain.
- **Quienes:** Whom/Who.
- **Químicos:** Chemicals.
- **Resguardado:** Sheltered.
- **Respectivas:** Respective.
- **Retiraron:** Retreated.
- **Sabio:** Wise.
- **Sacrifican:** Sacrifice.
- **Se dan cuenta:** realize.
- **Secreto:** Secret.
- **Seguridad:** Security.
- **Siglos:** Centuries.
- **Sitio:** Site.
- **Soldados:** Soldiers.
- **Sorpresivo:** Surprising.
- **Sufrimiento:** Suffering.
- **Sufrió:** Suffered.
- **Sus:** Your//Her/His/Its/Their.
- **Sustancia:** Substance.
- **Tecnología:** Technology.
- **Tenebroso:** Tenebrous.
- **Tentáculos:** Tentacles.
- **Tomaron:** They took.
- **Tope:** Top.
- **Transparente:** Transparent.
- **Treinta mil:** Thirty thousand.
- **Universo:** Universe.
- **Vastos:** Vast.
- **Vegetal:** Vegetable/Plant.
- **Violencia:** Violence.
- **Violetas:** Violets.

Questions about the story

1. ¿Cómo se llamaba el planeta en que vivían los asarianos?

    a.   Thessio.
    b.   Thessia.
    c.   Marte.
    d.   Pluton.

2. ¿Cómo obtenían su energía los asarianos?

    a.   De las estrellas.
    b.   De la luna.
    c.   De la galaxia.
    d.   Ninguna de las anteriores.

3. ¿Qué descubrieron los Asarianos?

    a.   Viajes en el tiempo.
    b.   El secreto del universo.
    c.   Viajar a la velocidad de la luz.
    d.   Ninguna de las anteriores.

4. ¿En dónde está situada la Ciudad Marfil?

    a.   En una Isla.
    b.   En una Montaña.
    c.   En un lago.
    d.   En un desierto.

5. ¿Qué recubre la Ciudad Marfil?

    a.   Un escudo.
    b.   El cielo.
    c.   Las estrellas.
    d.   Los árboles.

Answers

1.   A - What was the name of the planet on which the Asarians lived?
2.   A - How did the Asarians obtain their energy?
3.   B - What did the Asarians discover?
4.   A - Where is Ivory City located?
5.   A - What covers the Ivory City?

Chapter Sixteen

Basic Vocabulary

Fiesta de cumpleaños/Birthday Party

Gaby era una niña de **siete** años, que vivía en una linda y **amplia** casa en las **afueras** de la ciudad junto a sus padres y sus abuelos **paternos**. Pronto sería su **cumpleaños** número **ocho**, y estaba muy **emocionada**, ya que sus padres le **prometieron** que tendría una gran **fiesta** de cumpleaños, pero solo si tuviera buenas **notas** en el **colegio**.

Gaby era una niña muy dulce, **extremadamente inteligente**, y **aplicada**; y por esta razón ella era **sobresaliente** en la **escuela** y **obtuvo** las **mejores** notas de todo el **curso**. Sus padres y abuelos estaban muy **orgullosos** de ella, así que **decidieron** regalarle la gran fiesta de cumpleaños que ella quería. Para esta fiesta los padres de Gaby decidieron **alquilar**, **inflables**, **máquinas** de **palomitas de maíz,** juegos, **fuentes** de chocolate, un payaso y un **mago**. Todo se hizo en el gran **patio trasero** de la casa, el cual estaba **adornado** con **globos rosados**, blancos y rojos, también había **caballos** y **mariposas** por todos lados, ya que eran los animales favoritos de la niña.

Su mamá invitó a todos los niños que **estudiaban** con ella, en total fueron **quince** niños y niñas, todos se divertían, corrían, y comían **golosinas**. Los padres de los niños hablaban a un lado de la fiesta **prestando** mucha atención a sus pequeños. En ese **grupo** se **encontraba** una pequeña niña **llamada** Vicky, ella era un poco **tímida**, su naturaleza era ser **introvertida**, tristemente por ser tan **callada** **sufría** de *bullying*, otros niños la **rechazaban** y la hacían **sentir mal**. Vicky nunca **entendía** por qué la trataban así, regularmente era el **objetivo** de **bromas crueles** por los **demás** niños, y a pesar de que estaban en una fiesta de cumpleaños estas bromas crueles no paraban. Vicky fue a esta fiesta de cumpleaños **obligada** por su madre, ya que era la niña **nueva** de la escuela y no había podido hacer amigos, su madre al saber esto la llevó obligada a la fiesta, a pesar de los **pedidos** de su hija de no querer ir, igual la llevo.

Vicky en la fiesta se encontraba **sola**, su madre estaba **distraída** hablando con los otros padres, ella caminaba por la fiesta, no se subía a los inflables porque tenía **miedo** de **lastimarse** saltando, tampoco **disfrutaba** de los otros juegos o se acercaba al payaso, ya que este le daba miedo, solo encontró **algo** de diversión viendo al **mago** hacer lo suyo.

Al mismo tiempo, Gaby se divertía y disfrutaba **absolutamente** todo lo que en su fiesta de cumpleaños había. Lo primero que hizo fue saltar como loca en los inflables, jugaba con los demás niños para ver quién **llegaba** más alto, luego se dirigió a la **fuente** de chocolate donde se daba un **festín**.

Era el momento de **entregar** los **regalos**, Vicky sabía que Gaby fue una de las pocas que nunca le **molestó** en la escuela y siempre fue **amable** con ella, así que se **acercó** a ella para **felicitarla** y darle su regalo, pero rápidamente otros niños se acercaron y le dijeron a Gaby que no podría hablarle ni **juntarse** con Vicky porque si lo hacía ya no serían sus amigos. Gaby **al principio** no le hablo a Vicky y la ignoro.

Vicky quedó **devastada** y se fue a un **rincón** a **llorar**. Luego de un tiempo Gaby vio que la niña estaba sentada sola en un rincón, y no parecía divertirse ni disfrutar de la fiesta, Gaby se sintió terrible por lo que había hecho así que se acercó a ella, y comenzaron hablar, Gaby le pidió **disculpas** y la invitó a jugar en los múltiples juegos que se **hallaban** en la fiesta, la niña aceptó y pasaron el **resto** del cumpleaños jugando **juntas**. Cuando estaban jugando en el inflable, los otros niños se acercaron le **reclamaron** a Gaby que ¿**cómo** podía jugar con Vicky?, **sin titubear** Gaby les **respondió**, que ella era su amiga, y que no **permitiría** que la siguieran **tratando** mal, y así se fue a seguir jugando con Vicky. La madre de Gaby que había visto toda la situación desde el principio se sintió muy orgullosa del gran **corazón** de su hija, desde aquel día Gaby y Vicky se volvieron las mejores amigas.

Resumen de la historia

La historia de Gaby comienza con una niña que quiere celebrar su cumpleaños a lo grande. Para poder celebrar su fiesta de cumpleaños, debe sacar buenas notas en el colegio, y lo hace sin demasiado esfuerzo, por lo que sus padres la premian con la gran fiesta de cumpleaños que tanto deseaba. La fiesta estaba llena de globos de colores, fuentes de chocolate, inflables, un mago y un payaso. Todos los compañeros de clase de Gaby fueron a la fiesta. Todos jugaron, rieron y se divirtieron, excepto una niña tímida llamada Vicky. Por desgracia, los demás niños intimidan a la pobre niña por ser tímida y la nueva de la clase. Sus amigos obligan a Gaby a ignorar a Vicky, pero al ver lo mucho que sufre, Gaby la defiende y se convierte en su mejor amiga.

Summary of the story

The story of Gaby begins with a little girl who wants to celebrate her birthday in a big way. To have her birthday party, she must get good grades in school, and she does this without too much effort, so her parents reward her with a big birthday party that she wanted so much. The party was filled with colorful balloons, chocolate fountains, inflatables, a magician, and a clown. All of Gaby's classmates went to the party. Everyone is playing, laughing, and having fun except for a shy little girl named Vicky. Unfortunately, the other children bullied the poor girl for being shy and the new kid in the class. Gaby is forced by her friends to ignore Vicky, but when she sees how much she suffers, Gaby defends her and becomes her best friend.

Vocabulary List

- **Absolutamente:** Absolutely.
- **Acercó:** Approached.
- **Adornado:** Adorned.
- **Afueras:** Outside.
- **Al principio:** At the beginning.
- **Algo:** Something.
- **Alquilar:** Rent.
- **Amable:** Kind.
- **Amplia:** Broad/Wide.
- **Aplicada:** Applied.
- **Bromas:** Jokes.
- **Caballos:** Horse.
- **Callada:** Quiet.
- **Colegio:** School.
- **Cómo:** How.
- **Corazón:** Heart.
- **Crueles:** Cruel.
- **Cumpleaños:** Birthday.
- **Curso:** Course.
- **Decidieron:** They decided.
- **Demás:** Other.
- **Devastada:** Devastated.
- **Disculpas:** Apologies.
- **Disfrutaba:** Enjoyed.
- **Distraída:** Distracted.

- **Emocionada:** Excited.
- **Encontraba:** Find it at.
- **Entendía:** Understood.
- **Entregar:** Deliver.
- **Escuela:** School.
- **Estudiaban:** They studied.
- **Extremadamente:** Extremely.
- **Felicitarla:** Congratulate her.
- **Festín:** Feast.
- **Fiesta:** Party.
- **Fuente:** Fountain/Font/Source.
- **Globos:** Balloons.
- **Golosinas:** Candies.
- **Grupo:** Group.
- **Hallaban:** They found.
- **Inflables:** Inflatables.
- **Inteligente:** Smart/Intelligent.
- **Introvertida:** Introverted.
- **Juntarse:** Join.
- **Juntas:** Together.
- **Lastimarse:** Get hurt.
- **Llamada:** Call/Named.
- **Llegaba:** Arrived at.
- **Llorar:** Cry.
- **Mago:** Wizard/Magician.

- **Máquinas:** Machines.
- **Mariposas:** Butterflies.
- **Mejores:** Best/Better.
- **Miedo:** Fear.
- **Molestó:** bothered.
- **Notas:** Grades.
- **Nueva:** New.
- **Objetivo:** Target/Goal.
- **Obligada:** Forced.
- **Obtuvo:** Obtained.
- **Ocho:** Eight.
- **Orgullosos:** Proudly.
- **Palomitas de maíz:** Popcorn.
- **Paternos:** Paternal.
- **Patio trasero:** Backyard.
- **Pedidos:** Orders.
- **Permitiría:** Would allow.
- **Prestando:** Lend/Borrow/Pay.
- **Prometieron:** They promised.
- **Quince:** Fifteen.
- **Rechazaban:** They rejected.
- **Reclamaron:** Claimed.
- **Regalos:** Gifts.
- **Respondió:** Replied.
- **Resto:** Rest.
- **Rincón:** Corner.
- **Rosados:** Pink.
- **Sentir mal:** Feeling bad.
- **Siete:** Seven.
- **Sin titubear:** Without hesitation.
- **Sobresaliente:** Outstanding.
- **Sola:** Only/Lonely.
- **Sufría:** Suffered.
- **Tímida:** Shy.
- **Tratando:** Trying.

Questions about the story

1. ¿Cuántos años cumplió Gaby?

    a. 5
    b. 7
    c. 8
    d. 10

2. ¿De qué animales eran los adornos en la fiesta?

    a. Caballos y mariposas.
    b. Muñecas.
    c. Perritos.
    d. Princesas.

3. ¿Cómo se llama la niña que termina siendo amiga de Gaby?

    a. Cindy.
    b. Candy.
    c. Lulu.
    d. Vicky.

4. ¿Por qué los niños molestaban a Vicky?

    a. Por ser la nueva estudiante.
    b. Porque olía mal.
    c. Por vestirse raro.
    d. Ninguna de las anteriores.

5. ¿Cuántos niños fueron a la fiesta?

    a. 12
    b. 8
    c. 13
    d. 15

Answers

1. C - How old was Gaby?
2. A - What animals were the decorations at the party?
3. D - What is the name of the girl who ends up being Gaby's friend?
4. A - Why were the children bothering Vicky?
5. D - How many children attended the party?

Chapter Seventeen

Basic Vocabulary

Una hada nerviosa/A Nervous Fairy

Melanie es una chica de **quince** años **bailarina** de ballet, es la **chica** más **divertida** de su **grupo**, siempre hace **bromas** haciendo reír a sus compañeras y a su **maestra**, ella ama al ballet más que a **nada**, siempre es la **primera** en llegar y la **última** en **irse**. Es una excelente bailarina, **incluso enseña** a las niñas pequeñas del **curso** cuando la maestra le **pide ayuda**. Melanie puede ser un poco **distraída a veces**, pero es una buena **estudiante**, y una bailarina **extraordinaria**. Melanie gracias a sus **talentos ganó** una **beca**, ella es un gran **ejemplo** a seguir para sus **compañeras** y las niñas más pequeñas de la **academia** de ballet. Un día la maestra estaba preparando el **acto** tradicional de **fin del año**, y como era **diciembre** esta **fecha** era perfecta para que **actuaran** y **bailaran** la **obra** el cascanueces, y esa misma tarde la maestra daría a conocer que **roles** tendrían las chicas en el musical. Melanie fue la escogida para ser la **protagonista**. En esta obra tendrá el papel del **hada** de **azúcar**, Melanie no lo puede **creer**, estaba más que feliz y emocionada. La maestra le dice que por su trabajo y **constancia** se ganó este lugar.

Los días siguientes Melanie **ensayó**, día y noche. Al salir de la academia de ballet llega a su casa y sigue ensayando un poco más, ella quiere que todo le **salga** bien. El día del **acto** llega, y desde muy **temprano** comienzan los **preparativos**, el **teatro** se **condiciona** para la **obra**, llega el personal encargado de instalar los **Paneles** en el **fondo** del **escenario**, la maestra y otros **ayudantes adornan** el escenario, colocan un gran árbol de **Navidad**, **cuelgan** un gran **cascanueces**, ponen **copos de nieve**, para **ambientar** el lugar, otros van poniendo en los **asientos** números, para que al llegar los **espectadores**, sepan donde se pueden sentar.

Las bailarinas van llegando poco a poco, las más pequeñas están **disfrazadas** como copos de nieve, otras como **ratoncitos**, y el resto con sus disfraces y **trajes representando** a los **personajes** de la obra, las maestras ayudan a las más pequeñas, mientras que las más grandes se ayudan entre ellas para estar listas antes de la **presentación**. Melanie **siente** que la noche **anterior** casi no pudo **dormir** de la emoción, pero esto no le **afecta** en nada, ella se siente con mucha **energía**, y quiere salir lo más **pronto** a **escena**, ya los espectadores están en sus **respectivos puestos**, las **luces** se **apagan** y el show comienza. Salen los pequeños copos de nieve y comienzan a bailar, más adelante viene la escena de los ratoncitos y los **soldados**. La obra transcurre perfectamente, y poco antes de salir a bailar Melanie se llenó de nervios, esta es la primera vez que **se da cuenta** de que ella es la que tiene el **papel** más **importante**, y que todas las **miradas** estarán sobre ella.

La emoción del principio la hizo **olvidar** este **detalle**, y comienza andar de un **lado** a otro **llenándose** cada vez más de nervios. La maestra se acerca para decirle que se prepare, pues en pocos **minutos** saldrá a escena, y al ver a la chica le pregunta, "¿qué te pasa?", Melanie le responde, "es que estoy nerviosa".

La maestra **sonriendo** le dice, "no tienes por qué **temer**, todo saldrá bien solo tienes que bailar como siempre lo haces".

Melanie sale a escena, y una vez que **pisa** el escenario **recuerda** lo que su maestra le ha dicho, y solo **se deja llevar** por la música, al terminar ve que todos **están de pie aplaudiéndole**, y logra ver a su profesora que le **sonríe**, y allí acaba la obra. Al ir detrás de escena, todas sus compañeras y maestras, la reciben con un gran aplauso, la **felicitan** y la alaban diciendo que lo hizo increíble.

Resumen de la historia

Melanie es una sorprendente bailarina de ballet. Estudia en una distinguida academia de ballet clásico, que realiza el tradicional acto de fin de curso por ser la época navideña. El profesor de la academia decide recrear la obra clásica de este año, El Cascanueces. Melany consigue el papel protagonista, el dulce y bonita hada del azúcar. La niña se prepara y ensaya día y noche con constancia, ya que quiere que todo salga muy bien. Llega el día de la obra y los preparativos comienzan a primera hora de la mañana. El teatro está listo. Pronto el público está en sus asientos y comienza la presentación. Antes de salir al escenario, se pone nerviosa. Con la ayuda de su profesor, consigue controlar sus nervios. Sale y baila perfectamente. El público la ovaciona, y detrás del escenario, la profesora y sus compañeros la reciben con grandes aplausos llenos de alegría.

Summary of the story

Melanie is an astonishing ballet dancer. She studies in a distinguished classical ballet academy, which is making the traditional end of the year act because it is the Christmas season. The teacher of the academy decides to recreate this year's classic work, The Nutcracker. Melany wins the leading role, the sweet and pretty sugar fairy. The girl prepares and rehearses day and night with constancy since she wants everything to go very well. The day of the play arrives, and preparations begin early in the morning. The theater is ready. Soon the audience is in their seats, and the presentation starts. Before going on stage, she gets nervous. Thanks to her teacher, she manages to control her nerves. She goes out and dances perfectly. The audience gives her a standing ovation, and behind the stage, the teacher and her classmates receive her with big applause full of joy.

Vocabulary List

- **a veces:** Sometimes.
- **Academia:** Academy.
- **Acto:** act.
- **Actuaran:** Acting.
- **Adornan:** Adorn.
- **Afecta:** Affects.
- **Ambientar:** Ambient.
- **Anterior:** Previous.
- **Apagan:** Turn off/Off.
- **aplaudiéndole:** Applauding her.
- **Asientos:** Seats.
- **Ayuda:** Help.
- **Ayudantes:** Helpers/Assistances.
- **azúcar:** Suggar.
- **Bailaran:** They will dance.
- **Bailarina:** Dancer.
- **Beca:** Scholarship.
- **Bromas:** Jokes.
- **Cascanueces:** Nutcracker.
- **Chica:** Girl.
- **Compañeras:** Partners.
- **Condiciona:** Conditions.
- **Constancia:** Constancy/Perseverance.
- **Copos de nieve:** Snowflakes.
- **Creer:** Belive.
- **Cuelgan:** They hang.
- **Curso:** Course.
- **Detalle:** Detail.
- **Diciembre:** December.
- **Disfrazadas:** Disguised.
- **Distraída:** Distracted
- **Divertida:** Fun.
- **Dormir:** Sleep.
- **Ejemplo:** Example.
- **Energía:** Energy.
- **Ensayó:** Rehearsed.
- **Enseña:** Teaches.
- **Escena:** Scene.
- **Escenario:** Scenario.
- **Espectadores:** Spectators.
- **Están de pie:** Are standing.
- **Estudiante:** Student.
- **Extraordinaria:** Extraordinary.
- **Fecha:** Date.
- **Felicitan:** Congratulations.
- **Fin del año:** End of the year.
- **Fondo:** Background.
- **Ganó:** Won.
- **Grupo:** Group.
- **Hada:** Fairy.
- **Importante:** Important.
- **Incluso:** Also/Even.
- **Irse:** Leave/Go to.
- **Lado:** Side.
- **Llenándose:** Filling.
- **Luces:** Lights.
- **Maestra:** Teacher.
- **Minutos:** Minutes.
- **Miradas:** Looks.
- **Nada:** Nothing.
- **Navidad:** Christmas.
- **Obra:** Artwork/Play.
- **Olvidar:** Forget.
- **Paneles:** Panels.
- **Papel:** Paper/Role.
- **Personajes:** Characters.
- **Pide:** Ask for.
- **Pisa:** Step.
- **Preparativos:** Preparations.
- **Presentación:** Presentation.
- **Primera:** First.
- **Pronto:** Soon.
- **Protagonista:** Starring.
- **Puestos:** Seats.
- **Quince:** Fifteen.
- **Ratoncitos:** Little mouse.
- **Recuerda:** Remember.
- **Representando:** Representing.

- **Respectivos:** Respective.
- **Roles:** Roles.
- **Salga:** Goes out/Leave.
- **Se da cuenta:** Realized.
- **Se deja llevar:** Get carried away.
- **Siente:** Feel.
- **Sonríe:** Smile.
- **Sonriendo:** Smiling.
- **Talentos:** Talents.
- **Teatro:** Theater.
- **Temer:** Fear.
- **Temprano:** Early.
- **Trajes:** Suits/Costumes.
- **Última:** Last.

Questions about the story

1. ¿Qué es Melanie?

    a. Una bailarina.

    b. Una actriz.

    c. Una cantante.

    d. Una maestra.

2. ¿Qué papel obtuvo en la obra?

    a. El Cascanueces.

    b. El hada de azúcar.

    c. El hada madrina.

    d. Un copo de nieve.

3. ¿Qué obra actuaron en el acto de fin de año?

    a. La bella durmiente.

    b. La bella y la bestia.

    c. Anastasia.

    d. El cascanueces.

4. ¿Quién eligió a Melanie para ser la protagonista?

    a. La maestra.

    b. Sus compañeras.

    c. Un sorteo.

    d. Ninguna de las anteriores.

5. ¿Cómo se sentía Melanie antes de salir a escena?

    a. Feliz.

    b. Triste.

    c. Nerviosa.

    d. Molesta.

Answers

1. **A - What is Melanie?**
2. **B - What role did you get in the play?**
3. **D - Which play was performed at the year-end event?**
4. **A - Who chose Melanie to be the main character?**
5. **C - How did Melanie feel before going on stage?**

Chapter Eighteen

Valientes animalitos/Brave Little Animals.

Este **singular** grupo de animales nos van a llevar **a través** de una única y divertida historia. Max, Candy, Sue y Rex son amigos desde que todos eran **cachorros**. Max es un lindo **chimpancé**, Candy una dulce **suricata**, Sue una **intrépida gacela** y Rex un **noble jabalí**. Ellos viven en un hermoso y muy **lejano** lugar en las **profundidades** del hermoso continente **africano**, siempre **suelen meterse** en **aventuras** divertidas, y suelen hacer muchas **travesuras**. Una tarde mientras **descansaban al lado** de un gran **río** que **atravesaba** la **sabana**. Sue les dice que sería una gran aventura ir **más allá** del territorio que **habitan**, todos se miran con cara de **asombro** y **duda**, pues esas son tierras de grandes **depredadores**. Sue les dice que no tienen por qué **temer**, que ellos solo irán al **límite** del territorio y no más allá, al final **todos deciden** ir.

En el camino van hablando de lo que cada uno ha escuchado **sobre** lo que hay del otro lado de las tierras que habitan; Max comenta que sus papás le contaron que hay grandes depredadores, ellos **describen leones** con **garras** y **colmillos** gigantes que **cazan** todo lo que se **mueva**, Candy les dice que a ella le contaron que hay grandes **precipicios sin fondo** que **parecen infinitos** y que si **caen** nunca podrán salir, Rex comenta que su hermano le dijo que hay **extraños** animales muy **feos** y **extremadamente territoriales** llamados **Hipopótamos** que te pueden comer de un solo **bocado**, mientras Sue por su parte dice que nada le da miedo, y que si se llega a encontrar algo, ella le hará **huir** porque ella es muy fuerte, y si encuentran un precipicio lo saltara porque nadie es tan rápida y **ágil** como ella.

El viaje fue largo y **entretenido**, pero poco a poco que van llegando al límite, nuestros **simpáticos animalitos** cada vez se sienten más asustados, **presienten** que algo malo va a **pasar, sorpresivamente** al llegar al límite de las tierras, **nuestro** grupo de **exploradores**, no ven ni escuchar nada, no hay nada **mágico** ni **extraordinario**, solo **tierras áridas**. No había ni la más **mínima señal** de **vida** en aquel terreno. Sue **propone** ir más allá, pero Max se **niega rotundamente**, le dice que es muy peligroso y que desde un **principio** el **trato** era ir hasta el límite de las tierras, no más allá. Sue comienza a decir que él no quiere ir porque le da miedo, Max se **molesta** y le responde que no tiene miedo, pero es algo **estúpido retar** a la **suerte**, además **tampoco** quiere **exponerse** ni él ni sus amigos al peligro. Candy y Rex dan su opinión y tampoco están **de acuerdo** de ir más lejos. Sue se **da cuenta** de que ninguno de sus amigos quiere traspasar el territorio desconocido.

Sue tampoco quiere realmente, pero ella siempre quiere parecer la más **valiente**. Está a punto de decir que irá sola, ya que los demás no quieren ir, pero justo en ese momento se escucha un ruido **estruendoso** muy cerca de ellos. Por cosas del **destino** un árbol **viejo** y **podrido** se **rompe** y gran parte de él cae **súbitamente**, y la primera en salir corriendo es Sue. Cuando se **regresan** a su territorio, ríen a **carcajadas** por lo que Sue hizo. En este preciso momento llegan sus padres **preocupados**, y les preguntan qué ¿en dónde habían estado?, ya que hace un **rato** largo no los veían, Candy ya que no le gusta **mentir** les cuenta lo que hicieron. Sus padres se molestan y los regañan, les dicen que no pueden ir más allá de las tierras que ellos conocen, ya que del otro lado hay grandes depredadores, que les pueden hacer **daño**. El pequeño grupo se disculpa y promete que no lo volverán hacer, y a pesar del gran susto que se llevaron, Sue ya está pensando en cuál será su **próxima** aventura.

Resumen de la historia

Max, Candy, Sue y Rex son un grupo de animales divertidos y aventureros que nos llevan a vivir una aventura única y divertida. Un día estos amigos deciden ir a la frontera entre la tierra que habitan y la tierra donde las leyendas dicen que hay grandes depredadores. Cuando llegaron al lugar no había nada. Sue trató de convencer a los demás de que siguieran adelante, pero todos estaban en contra. Cuando de repente un fuerte ruido provocado por la caída de un viejo árbol hace que los pobres animalitos huyan asustados. Cuando vuelven a casa, todos se ríen, sobre todo de la reacción de Sue. Esperándolos estaban sus padres, que los reciben con una gran reprimenda por ir tan lejos a un lugar tan peligroso. Solo después de disculparse con sus padres, los pequeños prometen no ir tan lejos y mucho menos sin compañía. A pesar de todo, ya están pensando en cuál será su próxima aventura. ¿Qué les deparará el destino a nuestros exploradores?

Summary of the story

Max, Candy, Sue, and Rex are a group of fun and adventurous animals who take us on a fun and unique adventure. One day these friends decide to go to the border between the land they inhabit and the land where legends say there are large predators. When they arrive at the site they, there was nothing. Sue tried to convince the others to move forward, but they were all against it. When suddenly loud noise caused by the fall of an old tree makes the poor little animals run away scared. When they return home, everyone was laughing, especially at Sue's reaction. Waiting for them were their parents, who receive them with a big scolding for going so far away to such a dangerous place. Only after apologizing to their parents, the little ones promise not to go so far and much less without company. Despite all this, they are already thinking about what their next adventure will be. What will fate have in store for our explorers?

Vocabulary List

- **A través:** Across/Through.
- **Africano:** African.
- **Ágil:** Nimble/Agile.
- **al lado:** Nimble/Agile.
- **Animalitos:** Nimble/Agile.
- **Asombro:** Amazement.
- **Atravesaba:** Traversed/Crossed.
- **Aventuras:** Adventures
- **Bocado:** Snack
- **Cachorros:** Puppies/Cubs/Pups.
- **Caen:** Fall
- **Carcajadas:** Laughter.
- **Cazan:** Hunt.
- **Chimpancé:** Chimpanzee.
- **Colmillos:** Fangs.
- **Daño:** Damage.
- **De acuerdo:** Agree.
- **Deciden:** Decide
- **Depredadores:** Predators
- **Descansaban:** Rested
- **Describen:** Describe
- **Destino:** Fate/Destiny.
- **Duda:** Doubt
- **Entretenido:** Entertaining.
- **Estruendoso:** Thunderous.
- **Estúpido:** Stupid.
- **Exploradores:** Explorers.
- **Exponerse:** Expose.
- **Extraños:** Strangers.
- **Extraordinario:** Extraordinary.
- **Feos:** Ugly.
- **Gacela:** Gazelle.
- **Garras:** Claws.
- **Habitan:** Inhabit.
- **Hipopótamos:** Hippos.
- **Huir:** Flee.
- **Infinitos:** Infinite.
- **Intrépida:** Fearless.
- **Jabalí:** Wild boar.
- **Lejano:** Distant.
- **Leones:** Lions.
- **Límite:** Boundary.
- **Mágico:** Magical.
- **Más allá:** Beyond.
- **Mentir:** Lie.
- **Meterse:** Get in.
- **Mínima:** Mínimum.
- **Molesta:** Annoying/Upset.
- **Mueva:** Move.
- **Niega:** Denies.
- **Noble:** Noble.
- **Nuestro:** Our.
- **Parecen:** Seem.
- **Pasar:** Pass.
- **Podrido:** Rotten.
- **Precipicios:** Precipices.
- **Preocupados:** Worried.
- **Presienten:** They sense.
- **Principio:** Beginning.
- **Profundidades:** Depths.
- **Propone:** Proposes.
- **Próxima:** Next.
- **Rato:** Time.
- **Regresan:** Return.
- **Retar:** Challenge.
- **Río:** River.
- **Rompe:** Break.
- **Rotundamente:** Roundly.
- **Sabana:** Savanna.
- **Señal:** Signal.
- **Simpáticos:** Nice.
- **Sin fondo:** Bottomless.
- **Singular:** Singular.
- **Sobre:** On/Over/About.
- **Sorpresivamente:** Surprisingly.
- **Súbitamente:** Suddenly.
- **Suelen:** Usually.
- **Suerte:** Luck.

- **Suricata:** Meerkat.
- **Tampoco:** Also/Nor/Either/Neither.
- **Temer:** Fear.
- **Territoriales:** Territorial.
- **Tierras áridas:** Arid lands.
- **Todos:** All.
- **Trato:** Treatment.
- **Travesuras:** Mischief.
- **Valiente:** Brave.
- **Vida:** Life.
- **Viejo:** Old.

Questions about the story

1. ¿Cuál es el nombre de los cuatro amigos?

    a. Jose, Sue, Max, Rex.
    b. Sue, Maria, Candy, Rex.
    c. Candy, Rex, Max, Sue.
    d. Max, Rex, Sue, Coco.

2. ¿Quién sugirió ir a explorar?

    a. Sue.
    b. Max.
    c. Candy
    d. Rex.

3. ¿Qué sucedió cuando los animalitos volvieron al hogar?

    a. Jugaron.
    b. Comieron
    c. Los regañaron.
    d. Corrieron.

4. ¿Quién es la gacela?

    a. Rex.
    b. Max.
    c. Sue.
    d. Candy.

5. ¿A dónde querían ir los animalitos?

    a. A los límites del territorio.
    b. A los límites del país.
    c. A los límites del océano.
    d. A los límites del río.

Answers

1. **C** - What is the name of the four friends?
2. **A** - Who suggested going exploring?
3. **C** - What happened when the little animals returned home?
4. **C** - Who is the gazelle?
5. **A** - Where did the animals want to go?

Chapter Nineteen

El concierto de rock/The Rock Concert

Dimitri tiene un plan desde hace **mucho tiempo**, su **meta** es ir a ver su **banda** favorita Slipknot. Dimitri y sus **fieles** amigos **trabajaron** muy **duro**. Él trabajaba en una **compañía** de **construcción** como **ayudante**, al saber que Slipknot **vendría** a su ciudad se **propuso ahorrar** para poder **comprar** el **boleto**. Sus **deberes** en este empleo era **pintar paredes, reparar techos, pisos, colocar puertas** y **ventanas,** el dinero que ganaba con este empleo no era **suficiente**, así que buscó otras opciones, como **atender** en un **supermercado**, y **vender postres** a **domicilio**. Trabajó **honradamente** y con el **sudor** de su **frente** logro comprar los **deseados** boletos.

Dimitri está muy **contento**, pues ira a ver a su banda de rock favorita en **concierto**. Siempre quiso ver a esta banda, pero era muy **difícil** para él, ya que siempre fue un chico **humilde** y nunca le **alcanzaba** el dinero para una **entrada**, además que su ciudad no es muy popular ni importante así que **por lo general** las bandas de rock nunca la visitaban. Todo su grupo de amigos **también** reúnen el dinero para ir **juntos**. **Absolutamente** todos son **fanáticos** de esta banda y así como Dimitri, ellos también trabajaron duro para reunir el dinero, algunos trabajaron como **profesores sustitutos, fotógrafos,** y **mesoneros.**

La **mañana** del concierto Dimitri **despierta, desayuna,** se **baña,** se **viste** y sale hacer unas **cosas** que tiene **pendientes** antes de poder ir al concierto. **Planea** reunirse con sus amigos a las **seis y media de la tarde** en el **centro de la ciudad.** Dimitri llega y espera un **cuarto de hora** antes de que lleguen todos sus amigos, deciden ir a comer a un restaurante antes de ir al concierto, un amigo **sugiere** ir al restaurante donde él trabaja, ya que pueden darles un **descuento**. Después de quedar **satisfechos,** se dirigen a tomar un taxi para poder llegar **temprano** y así tener buenos **asientos, aunque** sus boletos no eran VIP, tenían una muy buena **vista** del escenario, pero antes de **entrar** al **recinto**, logran observar todos las **ventas** que se **encontraban afuera** del lugar, en la mayoría venden **mercancía** de las bandas que se presentaran hoy, **camisas, suéter, bolsos, gorros, discos, etc.** Todos deciden comprar algo. Entran al **estadio** buscando sus asientos, y aunque el **concierto** no ha empezado el recinto está a **reventar, casi treinta mil espectadores** esperando a ver la **mundialmente** famosa banda Slipknot, finalmente **consiguen** sus asientos, se sientan **cómodos** a hablar mientras el tiempo pasa.

Falta solo una **hora** para que el concierto comience, primero se presenta una banda **relativamente nueva** que **abrirá** el concierto para ellos, es muy conocida en la ciudad. Desde el primer momento que se **suben** al escenario demuestran todo su **talento y energía**, esta banda **suena realmente** bien y a muchos les gusta. Luego de que acaban su show, todos se preparan para recibir a la banda que estaban **esperando**, cuando se comienzan a escuchar los **golpes** a la **batería** y las otras **percusiones** que parecen **metralletas**, las guitarras empiezan a **retumbar acordes poderosos**, la **voz** del **vocalista** sonando **monstruosa** y melodiosa a la vez; y el **bajo** dándole **armonía** a todo el **conjunto**.

Es todo un **espectáculo**, hay **fuegos artificiales**, y **efectos especiales** con láser. Todos **enloquecen** empezando a **cantar, gritar, saltar** y **golpearse unos con otros,** Dimitri y sus amigos se sienten **atrapados** por la música. El estadio retumba con una de las **canciones** más conocidas, el **público** termina **aplaudiendo cansados** por el gran **despliegue** de energía, las **luces** se **apagan,** y la **multitud grita** que **toquen otra vez, coreando** en nombre de la banda, pero el show ha terminado. Es una **experiencia** única e **inigualable**, Dimitri se siente en otro mundo, y está más que feliz de vivir ese momento, luego de tres horas de show, Dimitri y sus amigos salen felices del concierto pensando que ahora tendrán una **anécdota** para en un **futuro**, contar a sus **hijos y nietos**.

Resumen de la historia

Dimitri, un joven de clase humilde, se entera de que su banda favorita estará en su ciudad dando un concierto. El joven y un grupo de amigos deciden trabajar duro para comprar entradas para ver a su banda favorita. Trabaja duro día tras día hasta que consigue reunir el dinero y comprar la entrada para ir al concierto con sus amigos. Cuando llegan al lugar del concierto, compran algunos recuerdos antes de entrar y, una vez dentro, comienza el espectáculo. Para abrir el espectáculo, toca primero un grupo muy conocido en la ciudad. Luego, finalmente, sale al escenario la esperada banda Slipknot. El espectáculo es increíble. Dimitri y sus amigos se van a casa contentos porque saben que han vivido una experiencia única que recordarán el resto de sus vidas.

Summary of the story

Dimitri, a young man of humble class, learns that his favorite band will be in his city giving a concert. The young man and a group of friends decides to work hard to buy tickets to see his favorite band. He works hard day in and day out until he manages to raise the money and buy the ticket to go to the concert with his friends. When they arrive at the concert site, they buy some souvenirs before going in, and once inside, the show begins. To open the show, a well-known band in the city plays first. Then finally, the long-awaited band Slipknot comes on stage. The show is incredible. Dimitri and his friends go home happy because they know they lived a unique experience that they will remember for the rest of their lives.

Vocabulary List

- **Abrirá:** Will open.
- **Absolutamente:** Absolutely.
- **Acordes:** Chords.
- **Afuera:** Outside.
- **Ahorrar:** Save.
- **Alcanzaba:** Reached/To be Enough.
- **Anécdota:** Anecdote.
- **Apagan:** Turn off/Off.
- **Aplaudiendo:** Clapping.
- **Armonía:** Harmony.
- **Asientos:** Seats.
- **Atender:** Attend.
- **Atrapados:** Trapped.
- **Aunque:** Although.
- **Ayudante:** Assistant.
- **Bajo:** Under/Bass.
- **Banda:** Band.
- **Baña:** Bath.
- **Batería:** Drummer.
- **Boleto:** Ticket.
- **Bolsos:** Bags.
- **Camisas:** Shirts.
- **Canciones:** Songs.
- **Cansados:** Tired.
- **Cantar:** Singing.
- **Centro de la ciudad:** Downtown.
- **Colocar:** Place.
- **Cómodos:** Comfortable.
- **Compañía:** Company.
- **Comprar:** Buy.
- **Concierto:** Concert.
- **Concierto:** Concert.
- **Conjunto:** Ensemble.
- **Consiguen:** Get.
- **Construcción:** Construction.
- **Contento:** Happy.
- **Coreando:** Chanting.
- **Cosas:** Things.
- **Cuarto de hora:** Quarter of an hour.
- **Deberes:** Homework/Duties.
- **Desayuna:** Breakfast.
- **Descuento:** Discount.
- **Deseados:** Desired.
- **Despierta:** Wake up.
- **Despliegue:** Deployment.
- **Difícil:** Difficult.
- **Discos:** Disks.
- **Domicilio:** Home.
- **Duro:** Hard.
- **Efectos especiales:** Special effects.
- **Encontraban:** Found.
- **Energía:** Energy.
- **Enloquecen:** Go crazy.
- **Entrada:** Enter.
- **Entrar:** Enter.
- **Espectáculo:** Show.
- **Espectadores:** Spectators.
- **Esperando:** Waiting.
- **Estadio:** Stadium.
- **Etc:** Etc.
- **Experiencia:** Experience.
- **Fanáticos:** Fans.
- **Fieles:** Faithful.
- **Fotógrafos:** Photographers.
- **Frente:** Front.
- **Fuegos artificiales:** Fireworks.
- **Futuro:** Future.
- **Golpearse:** Hit.
- **Golpes:** Hits.
- **Gorros:** Caps.
- **Gritar:** Shout.
- **Hijos:** Children.
- **Honradamente:** Honestly.
- **Hora:** Time.
- **Humilde:** Humble.

- **Inigualable:** Matchless.
- **Juntos:** Together.
- **Luces:** Lights.
- **Mañana:** Morning/Tomorrow.
- **Mercancía:** Merchandise.
- **Mesoneros:** Waiters.
- **Meta:** Goal.
- **Metralletas:** Machine guns.
- **Monstruosa:** Monstrous.
- **Mucho tiempo:** long time.
- **Multitud:** crowd.
- **Mundialmente:** Worldwide.
- **Nietos:** Grandchildren.
- **Nueva:** New.
- **Otra vez:** Again.
- **Paredes:** Walls.
- **Pendientes:** Pending/Earrings.
- **Percusiones:** Percussions.
- **Pintar:** Painting.
- **Pisos:** Floors.
- **Planea:** Plan.
- **Poderosos:** Powerful.
- **Por lo general:** Usually.
- **Postres:** Desserts.
- **Profesores sustitutos:** Substitute teachers.
- **Propuso:** Proposed.
- **Público:** Public.
- **Puertas:** Doors.
- **Recinto:** Site.
- **Relativamente:** Relatively.
- **Reparar techos:** Repair roofs.
- **Retumbar:** Rumble.
- **Reventar:** Burst.
- **Saltar:** Jump.
- **Satisfechos:** Satisfied.
- **Seis y media de la tarde:** Six-thirty in the evening.
- **Suben:** go up.
- **Sudor:** Sweat.
- **Suena:** Sounds.
- **Suéter:** Sweater.
- **Suficiente:** Enough.

- **Sugiere:** Suggests.
- **Supermercado:** Supermarket.
- **Talento:** Talent.
- **También:** Also.
- **Temprano:** Early.
- **Toquen:** Touch.
- **Trabajaron:** Worked.
- **Unos con otros:** With each other.
- **Vender:** Sell
- **Vendría:** Would come.
- **Ventanas:** Windows.
- **Ventas:** Sales.
- **Vista:** View.
- **Viste:** Viste.
- **Vocalista:** Vocalist.
- **Voz:** Voice.

Questions about the story

1. ¿A qué evento fue Dimitri?

    a. Una fiesta.

    b. Un concierto.

    c. Una Charla.

    d. A un funeral.

2. ¿Cómo consiguió el dinero de los boletos Dimitri?

    a. Trabajo Duro.

    b. Jugó Videojuegos.

    c. No hizo nada.

    d. Le regalaron los boletos.

3. ¿Con quién fue Dimitri al evento?/Who did Dimitri go to the event with?

    a. Con la novia.

    b. Con la familia.

    c. Con desconocidos.

    d. Con amigos.

4. ¿Cómo se llama la banda que fueron a ver?

    a. Slayer.

    b. Slapknot.

    c. Slipknot.

    d. Daft punk.

5. Cuál era el primer empleo de Dimitri?

    a. Ayudante en una compañía de teléfonos.

    b. Mesonero.

    c. Ayudante en un supermercado.

    d. Ayudante en una compañía de construcción.

Answers

1. **B - Which event did Dimitri attend?**
2. **A - How did Dimitri get the money for the tickets?**
3. **D - Who did Dimitri go to the event with?**
4. **C - What is the name of the band you went to see?**
5. **D - What was Dimitri's first job?**

Chapter Twenty

Una historia de amor/A Love Story

Hola me llamo Lexi, soy **estudiante** de **medicina** en una gran **universidad privada**. Es casi una **tradición** en mi familia estudiar en esta universidad, mis padres estudiaron allí. Fue en este sitio **donde** se **conocieron** y se **enamoraron**. Mi hermano **mayor** Christian estudia aquí también, es dos años mayor que yo, ya está en su último año de **ingeniería**. También estudian Lauren quien es la novia de mi hermano y mi mejor amiga; y Andy el mejor amigo de Christian, mi amor **platónico** . ellos estudian **leyes**. Sé muy bien que Andy me ve como la hermanita de su mejor amigo, además el tonto está enamorado de una chica **superficial, interesada** y **antipática** llamada Bárbara. Andy se enamoró de ella y la verdad es que no entiendo cómo ya que son totalmente **opuestos**. Andy es todo lo **contrario** a ella, afortunadamente el año pasado sus padres se la llevaron a un lugar **desconocido** de **vacaciones** y pensé que podría ser mi **oportunidad** para que Andy se **fijará** en mí, pero Bárbara es muy **astuta** y obviamente no iba a dejar a Andy tan fácil, mucho menos siendo el **heredero** de una gran **fortuna**.

Los padres de Andy murieron en un **accidente hace** tres años . Eran personas muy importantes, dueños de una gran fortuna que le **quedó** a Andy, y será **suya** cuando termine la universidad. Andy es la persona más linda y amable que puedan imaginar. Desde el accidente de sus padres los míos lo **acogieron** en mi casa; él pasa las **festividades** y vacaciones con nosotros. Mi familia no es como la de Andy, pero con mucha **honra** podemos decir que nos va bien. El amor y **comprensión** que Andy necesitaba lo encontró en mis padres, en mi hermano y en mí.

Un día estaba sentada en una **banca** cerca de un gran árbol, este es uno de mis lugares favoritos en la universidad, **de repente** alguien se sienta a mi lado y veo que es Andy. Mi corazón se **acelera de inmediato**. Él comienza a hablarme y yo lo noto un poco nervioso, le pregunto por qué y me dice que me quiere pedir un favor. Yo le digo que **por supuesto**, en qué le podría **ayudar**, lo que me pide me deja **confundida** y **enojada** al mismo tiempo. Él quiere que le ayude a ser más **romántico**, pues en **san Valentín** quiere hacer algo especial por Bárbara. Al principio quería **negarme**, pero él **literalmente** me **rogó** y no puedo dejar de ayudarle, así que terminé **aceptando**. Pensé que esta sería una mala idea y que podría salir **lastimada**.

Luego de a hablar con Andy me fuí a mi **dormitorio**, ahí me encontré con Lauren que me preguntó, "¿Qué has hecho?, ¿Dónde estabas?" Le comenté todo lo **sucedido** con Andy y ella me dijo, "¿Cómo puedes haber dicho que le ayudarás?, y yo le respondí, " No pude decirle que no", ya era tarde para **retractarme**.

Cuando íbamos camino al **comedor** ella me dijo que tenía una gran idea, yo estaría dos semanas sola con Andy ayudándole a ser más romántico, era el momento perfecto para hacer que se diera cuanta que yo era la chica para él y lo mejor es que Bárbara no estaría para **intervenir**.

Luego de comer me acerqué a Andy y le dejé unos **libros** para que los **leyera**, le dije que mañana empezarían nuestras **lecciones**. **Lo cité** en la misma banca junto al árbol, también le dije a Lauren que fuera, ya que quería ver la reacción de Andy. Ella estaría encargada de eso, y con ella también iría Cristian.Esto me pareció un **impedimento** para que Andy pudiera **expresarse,** pero igual lograría que me recitara un **poema**.

Andy me recitó un poema que pude ver **escogió al azar,** ni sabía que estaba diciendo. Cuando terminó yo le recité mi poema, al terminar vi las **distintas reacciones**. Lauren me miraba con cara de emoción. Cristian tenía cara de no entender nada, pero Andy quedó **seducido** por el poema. Vi como poco a poco se **acercaba** a mí para **besarme**, pensé que por fin llegaría el momento en el que podría besarlo, pero un grito de Cristian lo detuvo. Le gritó, "¿Qué haces?", Andy rápidamente se levantó y dijo que nada y ambos se fueron apresuradamente. Yo me quedé sola con Laurel quien me dijo que la **cara** de Andy era extraordinaria, y que si no fuera por Cristian me hubiese besado ahí mismo. Y así fue como las lecciones de romanticismo fueron **avanzando**. Hubo algunos momentos en los que Andy parecía querer darme un beso, abrazarme, y poco a poco fué cambiando, siendo más dulce conmigo. Incluso me enteré de que un día le preguntó un chico con el que salí porque habíamos terminado, yo solamente había tenido dos novios en la universidad y aunque muchos chicos estaban detrás de mí yo no había perdido la ilusión de que él se enamorara.

La noche antes del día de San Valentín preparé una última **clase** para Andy. Decidí que le diría todo lo que siento por él antes de que mañana fuera con Bárbara, pero esa noche Andy no apareció. Me sentí **frustrada, enojada** y **decepcionada**.

Al siguiente día Lauren me dijo que Andy salió muy temprano de la universidad y ni ella ni Cristian lo habían visto. El día pasó, en la tarde llegó Cristian; ellos Iban al **cine** me invitaron a ir con ellos, pero yo les dije que prefería ir sola al **muelle**. Me encanta este lugar.Estaba allí pensando en Andy y en cómo en este preciso momento debería estar con Bárbara, seguramente en una linda **cita** en un restaurant.. Estoy **concentrada** viendo las **olas** cuando siento una mano en mi hombro, al voltear veo Andy **frente** a mí. Yo solo logré preguntarle ¿ Qué haces aquí?, él me dijo que salió temprano para ver a Bárbara y decirle que ya no podían estar juntos, me **confesó** que durante estas dos **semanas** se dió cuenta de que yo era una persona muy cálida, linda y amorosa y que el pasar todo este tiempo junto a mí le ayudó a terminar de **darse cuenta** de que estaba enamorado de mí.

No pudo describir la emoción al escuchar esas palabras; simplemente le dije que yo también estaba enamorada de él. Me **arrojé** a sus **brazos**, Andy tomó mi cara entre sus manos y me recitó un bello poema. Yo me sorprendí y le dije que el poema era más que hermoso que habia jamás escuchado, él bromeó con que tuvo una gran profesora y me besó. Así fue como mi historia de amor comenzó.

Resumen de la historia

Andy le pide ayuda a Lexi, hermana menor de su mejor amigo que le enseñe a ser más romántico, Lexi esta secretamente enamorada de él y por eso no puede decir que no, por lo que decide ayudarlo. Su mejor amiga le dice que es el mejor momento para que pueda conquistar a Andy. Luego de las clases para aprender a ser más romántico, Andy se da cuenta de que se enamoró de Lexi, de su forma de ser y de su gran corazón.

Summary of the story

Andy asks Lexi, his best friend's younger sister, for help so she can teach him how to be more romantic, Lexi is secretly in love with him, and she can't say no, so she helps him. Her best friend tells her that this is the best time for her to make Andy fall in love. After the lessons to learn how to be more romantic, Andy realizes he is in love with her, because her big heart and the way she is.

Vocabulary List

- **Accidente:** Accident,
- **Acelera:** Accelerate.
- **Aceptando:** Accepting.
- **Acercaba:** Approaching.
- **Acogieron:** Welcomed/Receive.
- **Al azar:** Random.
- **Antipática:** Unfriendly.
- **Arrojé:** I threw.
- **Astuta:** Astute.
- **Avanzando:** Moving forward/Advance/Progress
- **Ayudar:** Help.
- **Banca:** Bench.
- **Besarme:** kiss me.

- **Brazos:** Arms.
- **Cara:** Face.
- **Cine:** Cinema.
- **Cita:** Date.
- **Clase:** Class.
- **Comedor:** Dining room
- **Comprensión:** Comprehension.
- **Concentrada:** Concentrated.
- **Confesó:** Confessed.
- **Confundida:** Confused.
- **Conocieron:** They met.
- **Contrario:** Contrary.
- **Darse cuenta:** Realize.
- **De repente:** Suddenly.
- **Decepcionada:** Disappointed.
- **Desconocido:** Unknown.
- **Distintas:** Different.
- **Dónde:** Where.
- **Dormitorio:** Bedroom.
- **Enamoraron:** Fell in love.
- **Enojada:** Angry.
- **Escogió:** Chose.
- **Estudiante:** Student.
- **Expresarse:** Express.
- **Festividades:** Festivities.
- **Fijará:** It will fix.
- **Fortuna:** Fortune.
- **Frente:** Front.
- **Frustrada:** Frustrated
- **Hace:** Ago/Made/Make.
- **Heredero:** Heir.
- **Honra:** Honor/Honour.
- **Impedimento:** Obstacle.
- **Ingeniería:** Engineering.
- **Inmediato:** Immediate.
- **Interesada:** Interested.
- **Intervenir:** Intervene.
- **Lastimada:** Hurt.
- **Lecciones:** Lessons.
- **Leyera:** Read
- **Leyes:** Laws.

- **Libros:** Book.
- **Literalmente:** Literally.
- **Lo cité:** Made an appointment.
- **Mayor:** Older/Greater.
- **Medicina:** Medicine.
- **Muelle:** Pier/Dock.
- **Negarme:** Refuse me.
- **Olas:** Waves.
- **Oportunidad:** Opportunity.
- **Opuestos:** Opposites.
- **Platónico:** Platonic.
- **Poema:** Poem.
- **Por supuesto:** Of course.
- **Privada:** Private.
- **Quedó:** To be/To stay.
- **Reacciones:** Reactions.
- **Retractarme:** Retract.
- **Rogó:** Beg.
- **Romántico:** Romantic.
- **San Valentín:** Valentine's Day.
- **Seducido:** Seduced.
- **Semanas:** Weeks.
- **Superficial:** Superficial.
- **Suya:** Yours.
- **Tradición:** Tradition.
- **Universidad:** University.
- **Vacaciones:** Vacation.

Questions about the story

1. ¿Qué favor le pidió Andy a Lexi?

    a. Le pidió que le enseñara a cocinar.

    b. Le pidió que le enseñara a cantar.

    c. Le pidió que le enseñara a besar.

    d. Le pidió que le enseñara a ser más romántico.

2. ¿Quién es Cristian?

    a. El novio de Lexi.

    b. El hermano de Cristian.

    c. El hermano de Lauren.

    d. El hermano de Lexi.

3. ¿Para quién quería Andy ser romántico?

    a. Para Barbara.

    b. Para Lauren.

    c. Para Lexi.

    d. Para Cristian.

4. ¿Qué le lee Lexi a Andy?

    a. Una canción.

    b. Un poema.

    c. Una carta.

    d. Nada.

5. ¿Con quién se quedó Andy al final?

    e. Lexi.

    f. Barbara.

    g. Lauren

    h. Cristian.

Answers

1. **D - What favor did Andy ask Lexi to do for him?**
2. **D - Who is Cristian?**
3. **A - Who did Andy want to be romantic for?**
4. **B - What does Lexi read to Andy?**
5. **A - Who did Andy end up with?**

Chapter Twenty - One

<u>Basic Vocabulary</u>

Una pequeña hechicera/A Little Sorceress

Esta no es la **típica** historia de un **mago** de la **Edad Media**, ya que se trata de un ser que **domina** la **magia**, pero no es un hombre sino una mujer, una **maga**, **hechicera** o como quieran llamarle. Cuando Teila **nació** parecía una niña normal, **común y corriente**. Hija de unos **campesinos** que no eran ni **pobres** ni **ricos**. La pequeña fue **creciendo**, pero a medida que crecía sus padres fueron viendo que Teila no era como los demás niños. Sus **poderes se desarrollaron** a medida que crecía. Entre ellos se destaca el poder entender y **controlar** a los animales para que hicieran lo que **ella quisiera**. Sus padres la **mantuvieron** en casa, no la dejaban ir muy **lejos** ni la llevaban con ellos a ningún lado, ya que temían que alguien viera lo que Teila hacía y la **descubrieran**. Si eso pasaba seguramente la terminarían **matando**, y aunque sus padres no entendían bien nada de lo que ella podía hacer ni el porqué de sus poderes, la amaban y sabían que la pequeña no era mala ni peligrosa

El **tiempo** pasó y Teila creció, sin haber ido nunca más lejos de su casa. Sus poderes también crecieron y muchas veces ella no sabía **controlarlos**. Un día llegó a su casa y **tocó** la **puerta** un hombre **misterioso** con un gran **bastón, barba** larga, y una **vestimenta** poco **usual**. Le dijo a Teila y a sus padres que venía a **llevarla** lejos, a un lugar donde iba a **aprender** y a controlar sus poderes, y ser una gran maga, que ese era su **destino**. Les explicó que era el Gran mago del norte. En el lugar donde vivían teila y sus padres existía la **leyenda** del Gran **mago** del **Norte**, de quién se decía vivía una gran montaña **lejana**. Les dijo que la noche en la cual Teila nació una **fuerza** poderosa la eligió para darle sus poderes. Desde que era pequeña, el mago habia **cuidado** de la joven desde las **sombras**. Había llegado la hora de que ella fuera a la tierra del mago a **desarrollar** sus poderes. Además una tarde en la que estaba en el **bosque** cerca de su casa, un **cazador** la había visto y le habia dicho a los demás **habitantes** que Teila era una bruja y en poco tiempo llegaron por ella.

Sus padres no tuvieron más **remedio** que dejarla ir con el mago. **Sabían** muy bien que si se quedaba la **matarían**. El mago les dijo que al llegar la **multitud** dijeran que allí no había ninguna **joven,** que solo vivían ellos dos y no tenían hijos. Así **arreglaron** todo, y el Mago con Teila **Partieron** a la tierra lejana.

Al llegar las personas a tocar su puerta, los padres **negaron** tener alguna persona más en su casa, los **aldeanos desconcertados** se fueron con el **pensamiento** de qué habría sido una **bruja** que estuvo por **aquí** y quedaron **alertas**. Teila y el gran mago llegaron a sus tierras, donde habitaban más seres como ella. Allí aprendió a desarrollar sus poderes y se convirtió en una gran maga que más tarde ayudaría a un gran **rey** a **recuperar** su **trono**.

Resumen de la historia

Teila es una joven que tiene poderes que no comprende muy bien y descubre que es una hechicera luego de que un misterioso hombre toca a su puerta. Este hombre era el gran mago del norte, el mago más poderoso de la edad media. Él le dijo a Teila y a sus padres que la joven tenía que ir con él a sus tierras pues allí aprendería a controlar sus poderes, y que de quedarse con sus padres los pondría en peligro. Así Teila se fue con el poderoso mago al norte. Allí aprendió a controlar muy bien sus poderes y se convirtió en una muy poderosa maga, cuyo destino sería ayudar a un importante rey a retomar el trono.

Summary of the story

Teila is a young girl who has powers she doesn't quite understand. After a mysterious man knocks on her door, she discovers she is a sorceress. This man was the great wizard of the north, the most powerful wizard of the Middle Ages. He told Teila and her parents that the young girl had to go with him to his lands because she would learn there to control her powers and staying with her parents would put them in danger. So Teila went north with the powerful wizard. There she learned how to control her powers very well and became a very powerful magician whose destiny would be to help an important king to retake the throne.

Vocabulary List

- **Aldeanos** : Villagers
- **Alerta:** Alert
- **Aprender** : Learn
- **Aquí** : Here
- **Arreglaron** : Fixed
- **Barba** : Beard
- **Bastón:** Cane
- **Bosque** : Forest
- **Bruja** : Witch
- **Campesinos** : Peasants
- **Cazador** : Hunter
- **Común y corriente:** Ordinary
- **Controlar** : Control
- **Controlarlos:** Controlling them
- **Creciendo:** Growing
- **Cuidado** : Care
- **Desarrollar** : Develop
- **Desconcertados** : Bewildered
- **Descubrieran:** Discover
- **Destino:** Destiny
- **Domina:** Dominates
- **Edad media:** Middle Ages
- **Ella:** she
- **Fuerza** : Force
- **Habitantes** : Inhabitants
- **Hechicera** : Sorceress
- **Joven:** Young
- **Lejana:** Distant
- **Lejos:** Far
- **Leyenda** : Legend
- **Llevarla** : Take her to
- **Maga:** Wizard
- **Magia:** Magic
- **Mago** : Magician
- **Mantuvieron** : Kept
- **Matando:** Killing
- **Matarían, :** They would kill,
- **Misterioso:** Mysterious

- **Multitud** : Crowd
- **Nació** : Born
- **Negaron** : Denied
- **Norte:** North
- **Partieron** : Departed
- **Pensamiento** : Thought
- **Pobres:** Poor
- **Poderes** : Powers
- **Puerta** : Door
- **Quisiera:** would like
- **Recuperar** : Recover
- **Remedio** : Remedy
- **Rey** : King
- **Ricos:** Rich
- **Sabían** : They knew
- **Sombras:** Shadows
- **Tiempo** : Weather / Time
- **Típica** : Typical
- **Tocó** : Touched
- **Trono:** Throne
- **Usual:** Usual
- **Vestimenta:** Attire.

Questions about the story

1. ¿Quién vino a buscar a Teila?

    a. El mago del sur.

    b. El mago del este.

    c. El mago del oeste.

    d. El mago del norte.

2. ¿Quién descubrió a Teila en el bosque?

    a. Un cazador.

    b. Un mago.

    c. Un pintor.

    d. Un pescador.

3. ¿Por qué Teila no se quedó?

    a. Porque la matarían.

    b. Porque la raptarían.

    c. Porque la abrazarían.

    d. Porque la cocinarían.

4. ¿Cómo se llamaba el mago?

    a. El mago del Norte.

    b. El guerrero malvado.

    c. El hechicero del norte.

    d. La bruja del sur.

5. ¿Cuál era el destino de Teila?

    a. Ayudar a un rey.

    b. Ayudar a una reina.

    c. Ser una guerrera.

    d. Ninguno de los anteriores

Answers

1. **D - Who came looking for Teila?**
2. **A - Who discovered Teila in the forest?**
3. **A - Why didn't Teila stay?**
4. **A - What was the magician's name?**
5. **A - What was Teila's destiny?**

Chapter Twenty-Two

Basic Vocabulary

La nueva reina/The New Queen

En un **reino antiguo** una reina dulce, quién era una gran **gobernante** murió por razones de **salud**. Está reina dejó tres **hijas,** la mayor llamada Catrina, la seguía Blair y la menor Cary. Al morir su madre una de ellas tendría que tomar su lugar, el gran **consejo** se reunió para **decidir**, ¿ Quién sería la **reina?** Luego de un largo debate se decidió que la **elegida** sería Cary. Ella tenía solo 16 años, pero al igual que sus hermanas desde niña fue **entrenada** para ser reina si este llegara a ser su destino.

El gran **consejo** le dió a **conocer** su **decisión** a las tres hermanas. Tanto Blair como Catrina, **felicitaron** a su hermana y le **brindaron** todo su **apoyo**, el gran **consejo** le dijo a Cary qué para tomar su lugar, primero tenía que ir a las **ruinas** y quedarse una noche allí para recibir **sabiduría** de los antiguos **maestros**. Todo esto debía ser antes del **solsticio** de **invierno**, que llegaría en 2 noches. El **viaje** hasta el sitio es de un día completo y no debería haber **inconvenientes ya** que era un viaje simple.

A Cary le **asignaron** dos de los mejores **guerreros** del reino, para que la acompañaran en su viaje. Se trataba de Erick y Seth, ellos habían sido los hombres de más **confianza** de su madre, y Cary se sentía segura junto a ellos. **Partieron** al día siguiente **rumbo** a las ruinas ubicadas lejos del **castillo** y la ciudad. El viaje iba tranquilo y en calma cuando en un momento salió una **flecha** disparada, la cual pasó muy cerca de Seth, rápidamente Cary y los guerreros corrieron buscando un sitio donde **protegerse**.

Seth se quedó con Cary, y Erik fue a **explorar** buscando a quiénes les había **atacado**. Luego de rato volvió con la chica y su compañero y les **informó** que quienes les habían atacado eran unos **mercenarios; cazadores** a quienes les pagaban para matar. Los tres estaban **confundidos**. ¿Qué hacían esos hombres en tierras del reino? Y ¿ Por qué querían **atacarlos?** En ese momento llegaron los mercenarios **acorralandolos**, les dijeron a los guerreros que solo querían a la **princesa** y si se la **entregaban** los dejarían ir **vivos**, los guerreros respondieron que tendrían que matarlos antes de entregar a Cary.

Los mercenarios se **lanzaron** al ataque, pero los guerreros estaban mejor **preparados** y eran más **astutos**. Comenzaron a luchar, en un momento casi **hieren** a Eric, pero Cary quién había tomado una **espada** y era una gran **espadachina**, lo salvo. Finalmente lograron **derrotar** a los cazadores. Seth interrogó a uno qué seguía vivo, le dijo que le **perdonaría** la vida si le decía quién los había **mandado** a por la princesa, la respuesta los dejó **fríos**, finalmente Cary completó su viaje y al volver a casa, le **contaron** todo lo que sucedió Catrina. Dijo que lo importante era que habían vuelto a salvo, pero el consejo decidió **investigar** quién quiso hacerle daño a Cary. Esta dijo que sabía quién había sido. En ese momento Erick y Seth **entraron** con el cazador que habían tomado **preso**, y de inmediato Cary se volvió a ver a su hermana Blair que estaba **pálida,** Cary la **enfrentó,** le dijo que el cazador había contado toda la **verdad**, y que ella fue quien les pagó para que la atacaran. En ese momento Blair **explotó** y confesó, que la que debería ser reina era ella; Cary decidió mandar a su hermana lejos del Castillo a vivir en el **exilio**, en un **campo** y con **compañía** para que cuidara de ella. Así Cary fue **coronada** reina. Reinó por muchos años con **sabiduría, comprensión, amor** y **tolerancia** tal como su madre lo había hecho antes.

Resumen de la historia

Un antiguo reino queda sin gobernante luego de que su querida reina muriera. El consejo se reúne y entre las tres hijas de la reina eligen a quien ocuparía el puesto. Carry la hija menor de las tres es la elegida, le dicen que debe ir fuera del reino a un lugar sagrado a buscar la sabiduría de los dioses. Acompañándola van dos fuertes guerreros, y todos emprenden viaje. Una gran aventura les espera cuando son atacados por mercenarios y cazadores, quienes habían sido enviados por una de las hermanas de Carry para así tomar el trono y ser ella la reina.

Summary of the story

An ancient kingdom is left without a ruler after its beloved queen dies. The council meets, and among the three daughters left by this queen, they choose who would fill the position. Cary, the youngest, is chosen to be the new queen. She must go outside the kingdom to a sacred place to seek for the wisdom of the gods. Accompanying her we find two strong warriors who set out on the journey. They were attacked by mercenaries and hunters who were sent by one of Cary's sisters to take the throne and become queen.

Vocabulary List

- **Acorralándolos:** Cornering them
- **Amor :** Love
- **Apoyo:** Support
- **Asignaron :** Assigned
- **Astutos:** Cunning
- **Atacado:** Attacked
- **Atacarlos:** To attack them
- **Brindaron :** Provided
- **Campo :** Country side
- **Castillo :** Castle
- **Cazadores :** Hunters
- **Compañía :** Company
- **Comprensión:** Understanding
- **Confianza :** Trust
- **Confundidos:** Confused
- **Conocer :** Know
- **Consejo :** Council
- **Contaron :** They counted
- **Coronada :** Crowned
- **Decidir:** Decide
- **Decisión :** Decision
- **Derrotar :** Defeat
- **Elegida:** Chosen
- **Enfrentó :** Confronted
- **Entraron :** Entered
- **Entregaba :** Delivered
- **Entrenado :** Trained
- **Espada :** Sword
- **Espadachín:** Swordsman
- **Exilio:** Exile
- **Explorar :** Explore
- **Explotó :** Exploited
- **Felicitaron :** Complimented
- **Flecha :** Arrow
- **Frío:** Cold
- **Gobernante :** Ruler
- **Guerreros :** Warriors
- **Hieren :** Wounded
- **Hijas, :** Daughters
- **Inconvenientes :** Inconvenient
- **Informó :** Reported
- **Investigar :** Investigate
- **Invierno:** Winter
- **Lanzaron :** Launched
- **Maestros:** Teachers
- **Mandado :** Sent
- **Mercenarios:** Mercenaries
- **Pálida:** Pale
- **Partieron :** They left
- **Perdonaría : Would** Forgive
- **Preparados :** Prepared
- **Preso:** Prisoner
- **Princesa :** Princess
- **Protegerse:** Protect
- **Reina:** Queen
- **Reino antiguo :** Ancient Kingdom
- **Ruinas :** Ruins
- **Rumbo :** Heading
- **Sabiduría :** Wisdom
- **Sabiduría:** Wisdom
- **Salud :** Health
- **Solsticio :** Solstice
- **Tolerancia :** Tolerance
- **Verdad:** Truth
- **Viaje :** Journey
- **Vivos:** Alive

Questions about the story

1. ¿Cuántas hijas dejó la reina?

    a. 2
    b. 4
    c. 3
    d. 5

2. ¿Quién era la hija mayor?

    a. Catrina
    b. Blair
    c. Cary
    d. Ninguna.

3. ¿Quién mandó a los cazadores atacar a Cary?

    a. Blair.
    b. Catrina.
    c. Seth.
    d. Otro.

4. ¿Quién eligió a Cary para ser reina?

    a. El consejo.
    b. Por voto.
    c. Nadie la eligió.
    d. Ninguno de los anteriores.

5. ¿Dónde tenía que ir Cary?

    a. A la playa.
    b. A la montaña.
    c. A las ruinas sagradas.
    d. Al templo sagrado.

Answers

1. **C - How many daughters did the queen leave behind?**
2. **A - Who was the eldest daughter?**
3. **A - Who sent the hunters to attack Cary?**
4. **A - Who chose Cary to be the queen?**
5. **C - Where was Cary to go?**

Chapter Twenty-Three

Basic Vocabulary

Conociendo la reina de Dinamarca/ Meeting the Queen of Denmark

Hola, **mucho gusto**. Mi nombre es Mario, el **capítulo** que les voy a **relatar**, es del día en que **accidentalmente conocí** a la **reina** de **Dinamarca**. Hace unos años yo estaba muy emocionado, quería **conocer Europa**. Nosotros en México tenemos el sueño de conocer Europa, cualquier país. Yo empecé a **ahorrar** cuando iba a la **preparatoria**, y cuando la terminé me fuí a trabajar a otro sitio aquí en México y después me fuí a conocer Europa. Conocí muchísimos países, todos me **encantaron**. Europa es increíble, es muy **rica** en **cultura** y uno de los países que no pensaba visitar era Dinamarca. Lo gracioso es que yo me moví **principalmente** en **tren** todo el tiempo. Me subía a los trenes para cambiar de ciudades o de países. Ahí está todo muy bien **conectado**.

Uno de los trenes a los que me **subí** iba a **pasar** por Dinamarca donde tenía que hacer una **escala** de alrededor de 7 u 8 horas; y en vez de quedarme **solamente** en la **estación** de tren por ocho **horas**, decidí **salir** a pasear. No tenía planeado nada, preguntarle a la gente que vive ahí fue muy **sencillo**. Solo les pregunté qué había para hacer **cerca** de la estación y me **indicaron**. Me llevaron al **Museo** de **Historia** de Dinamarca, que por **suerte** se **encontraba** cerca. Cuando **llegué** no había nadie. Quizá era muy **temprano**. Entré y cuando iba a pagar me dijeron que ese día era **gratis**. Justo solo ese día. Me pareció increíble.

No pregunté más y me pasé todo el día, bueno... unas horas en el museo. Había cosas muy **interesantes para ver**. Los **daneses** como todos los países, tienen una cultura muy **rica** y terminando ya estaba yo muy **cansado** y tenía mucha hambre. Pensé que tenía que usar algo de mis ocho horas para comer. Cuando ya iba de salida, quizá unas tres o cuatro horas después, me di cuenta que había una **alfombra** roja desde la **calle** hasta la **entrada** al museo.

La alfombra roja, no sé si saben, se usa normalmente para la **realeza** o para la gente muy importante, los **artistas**. Y me dije " Esto es extraño" Me están dando muy bien la **bienvenida** quizá los daneses, porque en verdad era la única persona que estaba allí. En el museo no **había nadie** más. Quizá me crucé con una o dos otras personas, no más. Entonces le fuí a **preguntar** al de la entrada ¿ **Qué** es lo que está pasando y **por qué** hay una alfombra roja ahí?

Me dijo "¡**Oye**! ¿ No sabes?"

Y yo: "Pues no, por eso te estoy preguntando"

Hoy se **inaugura** una parte del museo . Lamentablemente ya no recuerdo que parte era, pero era relativa a un momento **antiguo** de la historia de los daneses. Fué algo muy bonito porque me acuerdo perfecto de que fué el **salón**, o uno de los salones que más me gustó; y no solo eso, me siguió **platicando**, "Pues sí, es que va a venir Margarita", "¿Margarita?" me parece que sí es Margarita, ya no recuerdo. Espero no estar diciendo **mentiras**. Pero bueno, me dijo solamente el nombre de una mujer. A lo cual me quedé con **cara intrigada** y sin saber qué hacer.

Claramente esta persona se **empezó** a reír y me preguntó "¿No sabes **quién** es ella, verdad?", y yo "Pues no, pero si me puedes platicar me encantaría". **Resulta** que la **reina** de Dinamarca iba a ser la que iba a inaugurar esa **sala**. El **evento** iba a comenzar unas tres o cuatro horas después de que yo ya me iba a ir.

Tenía que **agarrar** un tren, pero dije, "¿**Cuántas** veces puedes conocer a la reina de un país en donde **ni siquiera** sabías que había reina?" Fue algo muy interesante y muy divertido, porque **decidí** pues **quedarme** ahí, **mori** un poco de hambre. Pero me senté en una banca ahí, justo **afucra** del museo. **De repente** empezó a llegar un poco más de gente, principalmente **fotógrafos** y **reporteros**.

Uno se puede **dar cuenta**, porque es muy fácil **distinguirlos** ¿ No? Pues con sus **cámaras** y gente que viene muy **apresurada**. **Eventualmente** llegó una **limusina** muy, muy, muy, muy grande. Se **bajaron** como ocho personas vestidas de negro, **sacos** negros, **corbatas** negras, **camisa** blanca, entrando muy rápido como haciendo un **análisis** del **lugar**.

Luego baja una persona ya de **mayor edad**. **Obviamente**, yo me acerqué muy rápido, **sin causar** problemas, y me empecé a **tomar** un **montón** de selfis con la reina. Y así es como conocí a la reina de Dinamarca. En realidad no la conocí pues no hablé con ella, no iba a hablar con ella. Además, y aunque hablaba inglés, no me iba a **atrever** a hacerlo con la reina.

¡Seguramente no hablaba español! Tuve que esperar un poco más para que **dieran** la inauguración oficial. La inauguración oficial estuvo muy bonita aunque yo no hablo danés. Había muchísima **gente**, muchísimas **sillas**. La reina dio un **discurso** con una hermosa **plática** de la que obviamente no entendí nada por qué estaba en danés y yo no lo hablo, pero fue muy divertido y muy bonito, fue muy **apasionado**. No necesitas hablar un idioma para entender las **reacciones** y las emociones de la gente. Después de eso ¿ Recuerdan que yo estaba muriendo de hambre? **Después** hubo un **festín** en **conmemoración** de la inauguración con **platillos** típicos de esa época en Dinamarca.

Fue increíble. Había **cerdo**. ¿Se imaginan un cerdo justo ahí, con la **manzana** en la **boca**? Había una especie de **maíz** danés, que fue lo que me trataron de explicar. Me regalaron muchísimas bebidas entre **vino** o lo que yo creía que era vino, y **cerveza**. Fue un festín delicioso. Para ese entonces, yo ya tenía que estar en la estación de tren.

Pero decidí, " "De ninguna manera". No todos los días conoces a la reina de Dinamarca y te brindan un festín **gigante**, y delicioso. Me puse a charlar con muchos de los presentes. Les pareció muy divertido que yo, siendo **mexicano**, estuviera en esa inauguración ese día. Pero así son las cosas. La suerte te lleva a **distintos** lugares. Ya terminando el evento, obviamente volví a la estación, les puse **carita** de "Oigan, perdón creo que no llegué, solo vengo tres horas **tarde**". Los daneses son personas muy **amables**.

Me dijeron, "¿En verdad **perdiste** el tren?" Sí, "Bueno, está bien, te lo **repondré**". Solamente tienes una pequeña **tarifa** de **cambio** por unos cuantos euros. Gracias al **cielo** no fue el precio **completo,** porque hubiera sido mucho más caro. Solo pagué esa perqueña tarifa y me fuí muy feliz con muchísimas **fotos** con la reina de Dinamarca.

A mí me encanta **contar** esta historia y siempre lo hago como ahora, cómo conocí a la reina de Dinamarca y la gente se emociona. Claramente esto para mí fué una experiencia **inolvidable**. Esto me pasó hace más de 12 años, pero sigo teniéndola en mi **corazón**.

Resumen de la historia

Un joven mexicano llamado Mario viaja a Dinamarca para cumplir su sueño de visitar Europa, recorre muchos sitios en tren. Un día le pide a un local que le ayude a encontrar un lugar para visitar, esa persona le señala un museo. Él, encantado se dirige a descubrir un poco de la historia de ese hermoso país; sin saber el que ese día conocería la Reina del país..

Summary of the story

A young Mexican man named Mario travels to Denmark to fulfill his dream of visiting Europe. He travels many places by train. One day he asks a local to help him find a place to visit, that person points him to a museum. He was delighted to discover a bit of the history of this beautiful country. He didn't know he would meet the Queen of Denmark that day.

Vocabulary List

- **Accidentalmente:** Accidentally
- **Afuera:** Outside
- **Agarrar:** Grab
- **Ahorrar:** Save
- **Amables:** Kind
- **Análisis:** Analysis
- **Antiguo:** Former
- **Apasionado:** Passionate
- **Apresurada:** Rushed
- **Artistas:** Artists
- **Atrever:** Dare
- **Bajaron:** Bajaron
- **Bienvenida:** Welcome
- **Boca:** Mouth
- **Calle:** Street
- **Cámaras:** Cameras
- **Cambio:** Change
- **Camisa:** Shirt
- **Cansado:** Tired
- **Capítulo:** Chapter
- **Cara:** Face
- **Carita: Little** Face
- **Alfombra:** Carpet
- **Causar:** Cause
- **Cerca:** Fence
- **Cerdo:** Pig
- **Cerveza:** Beer
- **Cielo:** Sky
- **Cierto:** True
- **Claramente:** Clearly
- **Compartimos:** We share
- **Completo:** Completely,
- **Conectado:** Connected
- **Conmemoración:** Commemoration
- **Conocer:** Meet
- **Conocí:** I met
- **Contar:** Count
- **Corazón:** Heart
- **Corbatas:** Ties
- **Cuántas:** How many
- **Cultura:** Culture
- **Daneses:** Danish people
- **Dar cuenta:** Give notice
- **De repente:** Suddenly
- **Decidí:** I decided
- **Después:** Later
- **Dieran:** Give
- **Dinamarca:** Denmark
- **Discurso:** Speech
- **Distinguirlos:** Distinguish them
- **Distíntos:** Distinguish them
- **Edad:** Age
- **Empezó:** Started
- **Encantaron:** Enchanted
- **Encontraba:** Found
- **Entrada:** Entrance
- **Escala:** Scale
- **Estación:** Station
- **Europa:** Europe
- **Evento:** Event
- **Eventualmente:** Eventually
- **Festín:** Feast
- **Fotógrafos:** Photographers
- **Fotos:** Photos
- **Gente:** People
- **Gigante:** Giant
- **Gratis:** Free
- **Había:** There was
- **Historia:** History/Story.
- **Horas:** Hours
- **Inaugura:** Inaugurated
- **Indicaron:** Indicated
- **Inolvidable:** Unforgettable
- **Interesantes:** Interesting
- **Intrigada:** Intrigued
- **Justo:** Just / right on...

- **Limusina:** Limousine
- **Llegué:** I Arrived
- **Lugar:** Place
- **Maíz:** Corn
- **Manzana:** Apple
- **Mayor:** Major
- **Mentiras:** Lies
- **Mexicano:** Mexican
- **Montón:** A lot, a bunch of...
- **Morí:** I died (I was dying to eat)
- **Mucho gusto:** Pleased to meet you
- **Museo:** Museum
- **Nadie:** Nobody
- **Ni siquiera:** Not even
- **Obviamente:** Obviously
- **Oye:** Hey
- **pago:** Paid
- **Pasar:** Go to
- **Perdiste:** Lost
- **Plática /conversación. The word "plática" is used only in Mexico:** Chat
- **Platicando / conversando:** Chatting
- **Platicar / conversar:** Chatting
- **Platillos:** Dishes
- **Por qué:** Why
- **Preguntar:** Ask
- **Preparatoria:** High School
- **Principalmente:** Mainly
- **Qué:** What
- **Quedarme:** Stay
- **Quién:** Who
- **Reacciones:** Feedback/Reaction
- **Realeza:** Royalty
- **Reina:** Queen
- **Repondré:** I will replenish
- **Reporteros:** Reporters / Journalists
- **Resulta:** Turns out
- **Rica:** Rich
- **Rico:** Rich
- **Sacos:** Jackets
- **Sala:** Room
- **Salir:** Exit

- **Salón:** lounge/exhibition room
- **Sencillo:** Simple
- **Sillas:** Chairs
- **Sin:** Without
- **Solamente:** Only/just
- **Subí:** Upload/climb
- **Suerte:** Luck
- **Tarde:** Afternoon
- **Tarifa:** Rate
- **Temprano:** Early
- **Tomar:** Take
- **Tren:** Train
- **Vino:** Wine

Questions about the story

1. ¿ Qué país visitó Mario?

   a. Suecia.

   b. Suiza.

   c. Noruega.

   d. Dinamarca.

¿ Qué lugar visitó Mario?

   a. Museo.

   b. Biblioteca.

   c. Restaurant.

   d. Estadio.

¿Para quién era la carpa roja?

   a. Para un cantante.

   b. Para un rey.

   c. Para una Reina.

   d. Para él.

¿En qué le gustaba viajar a Mario?

   a. En avión.

   b. En autobús.

   c. En auto.

   d. En tren.

¿Qué hizo por último Mario?/

   a. Comer.

   b. Hablar con la Reina.

   c. Visitar el Museo.

   d. Ninguno de los anteriores.

Answers

   1. **D - What country did Mario visit?**

   2. **A - What place did Mario visit?**

   3. **C - Who was the red tent for?**

   4. **D - What did Mario like to travel in?**

   5. **A - What did Mario do last?**

Chapter Twenty-Four

Basic Vocabulary

Fanático a la adrenalina/Adrenaline Fanatic

Mi nombre es Daniel y les **contaré** un **evento** que sucedió hace cinco años. Una noche estaba pensando en salir en **bicicleta**, y se me **ocurrió** la **idea** de ir a una **montaña** que estaba aproximadamente a   dos horas de mi casa. Tenía planeado ir la mañana siguiente. No conocía muy bien ese lugar porque solo había ido **una vez**, esto me **motivó aún** más. Salí muy temprano al día siguiente, y después de dos horas, llegué a la montaña.

Antes de **subir revisé** mis cosas y mi bicicleta, todo estaba en perfectas **condiciones** para mi **aventura**. Lamentablemente ninguno de mis amigos pudo **acompañarme**, ya que tenían cosas que hacer ese día. Tenía **planeado** tomar el mismo camino que había tomado una vez, ya que era lo único que conocía. Al pasar 30 minutos, ya había subido una gran parte de la montaña y me **detuve** un **rato** a **descansar** y **beber agua**.

A lo lejos ví otra montaña que parecía estar más **interesante** que esta que estaba **escalando** y como aún era temprano, dije ¿Por qué no? Voy a ir a **explorar** aquella. Así que decidí **salirme** de mi **ruta** hasta llegar a la siguiente montaña. Al llegar, noté que era más **empinada** y el camino era mucho más **difícil**, pero aún así empecé a subir.

Tardé **alrededor** de una hora o una hora y media; no recuerdo bien. Fué **agotador**. Me detuve en la **cima** y revisé **de nuevo** mi bicicleta. **Noté** que un **pedal** estaba **flojo** y traté de **arreglarlo**. Al cabo de unos minutos parecía que ya estaba bien **ajustado**, por lo que decidí empezar el **descenso**.

Al instante noté que esta ruta era algo **complicada** y peligrosa, así que empecé a tomar mis **precauciones** y bajar un poco más **despacio**. Logré bajar bien una parte de la montaña, pude **descansar** en un lugar y **analizar** el camino que debía tomar para seguir mi descenso. Después de unos minutos decidí tomar el camino que me pareció más fácil, pero al instante, cuando estaba bajando noté que mi bicicleta no estaba muy bien. La sentí algo floja, pero no podía **detenerme**, porque podría ser **peligroso** y podía **resbalar**.

Iba bastante rápido, tanto que mi corazón **latía** muy fuerte y rápido, la **adrenalina** corría por mis **venas**. Era una emoción muy fuerte que me encantaba. Vi que adelante había una curva muy cerrada, con bastantes **piedras** y un camino muy **irregular**. Empecé a bajar la velocidad y prepararme. Logré tomar bien esa curva y salir **ileso**. Pero me esperaba una más grande. Entonces tuve que girar bastante rápido. Tomé el **control** con fuerza y pude salir de esta.

Cuando pensé que todo había pasado estuve a punto de **caer**, pues pasé por encima de una roca muy grande y esta me **descontroló**. No sé cómo pude tomar el **equilibrio** de nuevo, pero al final lo **logré**. Ya eran muchas emociones para ese rato, pero eso no se **comparó** con lo que **vendría** después. Ya había bajado de esa montaña y solamente tenía que tomar mi ruta y regresar a casa, pero algo dentro de mí quería más.

Así que tomé otra ruta, una nueva, lo que sería un **grave** error. Parecía bastante sencilla. La única diferencia era que esta se veía más larga, ya que tenía que **rodear** mucho terreno. Una vez más revisé mi bicicleta, pero no pude encontrar la **falla**. Tomé la mala decisión de **arriesgarme** y bajar por esa nueva ruta. Todo iba muy bien, parecía muy sencillo aunque cada vez tomaba más y más velocidad; **provocando** que **perdiera** el control.

Me asusté y quise **frenar**, pero cuando lo hacía mi **llanta trasera** derrapaba. **Me asusté** mucho porque mi única opción era lograr bajar hasta el **asfalto** pero aún faltaba muchísimo, y no sabía si lo **lograría**. Por el camino irregular tuve un pequeño **salto**, el cual me descontroló completamente y que causó que mi bicicleta se **partiera**. Solo recuerdo que salí **volando**, y **caí**. Me dí un golpe muy fuerte y creo que me **desmayé**. Al despertar me dolía mucho una **pierna** y la **cabeza**.

Quise **levantarme**, pero no pude. Creo que tenía **fracturada** la pierna.. Pude ver mi bicicleta partida en dos. Lo primero que quise hacer fue **llamar** pero no tenía mi **celular**, .Estaba muy mal. No podía caminar, ni siquiera **arrastrarme**. Temí que nadie me encontrara ya que esa **área** es muy poco **habitada**. Me **desesperé** y empecé a **gritar**. Pero nadie me **escuchaba**, ahí estuve alrededor de dos horas hasta que se me ocurrió **rodar** un poco, pero no fue muy buena idea, ya que las **costillas** también me **dolían** mucho.

Cuando abrí los ojos vi que un **extraño** estaba **frente** a mí y me preguntaba cómo me sentía. No podía **verlo** muy bien ya que tenía la **visión borrosa**. Él me dijo que lo esperara, que iría por **ayuda**. Cuando pasó un rato llegó un **paramédico** junto con más personas y el extraño; y me bajaron de la montaña. Por suerte esa persona vivía cerca de ahí y todos los días hacía ese recorrido.

Él me dijo que se asustó mucho cuando me vió, ya que pensaba que estaba **muerto**. Se sorprendió porque vió la bicicleta hecha pedazos. Por **fortuna** solo fueron unas cuantas fracturas. El extraño se llamaba José y también **encontró** mi celular, el cual muy **amablemente** me entregó. Yo le dije que estaba muy

agradecido, me había salvado la vida. José solo sonrió y me dijo que tuviera más **cuidado** en un futuro. Incluso le dije que cuando me **recuperara** y comprara otra bicicleta volvería a intentarlo, todos nos reímos. Obviamente les dije que solo era una broma.

Ese fue el primer gran **accidente** que tuve en mi vida y espero que sea el último, aunque esa experiencia me **marcó** para siempre. Hace poco tiempo regresé al lugar, pero esta vez caminando. Quería **recorrerlo** y ver exactamente dónde **caí**, cuando ví detaladamente el lugar, supe la suerte que me acompañó ese día y en ese momento me di cuenta de lo peligroso que era realmente.

Resumen de la historia

Daniel es un joven aventurero fanático de la adrenalina, tiene como pasatiempo conducir bicicletas, un día con ganas de explorar se va a una montaña conocida. Pero tiene hambre por aventura, así que recorre caminos no explorados. Aunque poco a poco él siente que la bicicleta no responde como lo hace habitualmente, sigue conduciendo a gran velocidad. Cada vez busca retos más peligrosos, luego se dirige a una montaña que desconocida, que le llamó la atención. Manejó por caminos peligrosos y cuando decidió regresar, tuvo un accidente que lo dejó en muy mal estado. Era un lugar muy solitario y tenía miedo de morir allí. Por suerte un desconocido pasó y le salvó la vida.

Summary of the story

Daniel is a young adventurous fanatic of adrenaline, his hobby is riding bicycles. One given day, wanting to explore, he goes to a well-known mountain. But he is hungry for adventure, so he rides on unexplored roads. Although he gradually feels the bike´s performing differently, he continues to ride at high speed. He looks for more and more dangerous challenges, then he heads to a mountain he didn't know, but it caught his eye. He rode fast on dangerous roads and when he was ready to return he had an accident that left him in a serious condition. It was a lonely place and he was afraid of dying there. Luckily a stranger passed by and saved his life.

Vocabulary List

- **Accidente:** Accident.
- **Acompañarme:** Join me.
- **Adrenalina:** Adrenaline.
- **Agotador:** Exhausting.
- **Agradecido:** Grateful.
- **Agua:** Water.
- **Ajustado:** Tight.
- **Alrededor:** Around.
- **Amablemente:** Kindly.
- **Analizar:** Analyze.
- **Área:** Area.
- **Arrastrarme:** Drag myself.
- **Arreglarlo:** Fix it.
- **Arriesgarme:** Risk me.
- **Asfalto:** Asphalt.
- **Aventura:** Adventure.
- **Ayuda:** Help.
- **Beber:** Drink.
- **Bicicleta:** Bicycle.
- **Borrosa:** Blur.
- **Cabeza:** Head.
- **Caer:** Fall.
- **Caí:** I fell.
- **Celular:** Cell phone.
- **Cima:** Top.
- **Comparó:** Compared.
- **Complicada:** Complicated.
- **Condiciones:** Conditions.
- **Contaré:** I will tell.
- **Control:** Control.
- **Costillas:** Ribs.
- **Cuidado:** Care.
- **De nuevo:** Again.
- **Descansar:** Rest.
- **Descenso:** Descent.
- **Descontroló: Got himself** out of control.
- **Desesperé:** Despaired.
- **Desmayé:** Fainted.
- **Despacio:** Slowly.
- **Detenerme:** Stop.
- **Detuve:** Stopped.
- **Difícil:** Difficult.
- **Dolían:** Hurt.
- **Empinada:** Steep.
- **Encontró:** Found.
- **Equilibrio:** Balance.
- **Escalando:** Climbing.
- **Escuchaba:** Listened.
- **Evento:** Event.
- **Explorar:** Explore.
- **Extraño:** Strange.
- **Falla:** Failure.
- **Flojo:** Sluggish.
- **Fortuna:** Fortune.
- **Fracturada:** Fractured.
- **Frenar:** Brake.
- **Frente:** Forehead.
- **Grave:** Serious.
- **Gritar:** Shout.
- **Habitada:** Inhabited.
- **Ileso:** Unharmed.
- **Interesante:** Interesting.
- **Irregular:** Irregular.
- **Latía:** was beating
- **Levantarme:** Get up.
- **Llamar:** Call.
- **Llanta:** Tire.
- **Lograría:** Would make it.
- **Logré:** Made it.
- **Marcó:** Dialed.
- **Me asusté:** I got scared.
- **Montaña:** Mountain.
- **Motivó:** Motivated.
- **Muerto:** Dead.
- **Noté:** I noticed.
- **Ocurrió:** Occurred.
- **Paramédico:** Paramedic.
- **Partiera:** Break/Left.

- **Pedal:** Pedal.
- **Peligroso:** Dangerous.
- **Perdiera:** Lost.
- **Piedras:** Stones.
- **Pierna:** Leg.
- **Planeado:** Planned.
- **Precauciones:** Precautions.
- **Provocando:** Causing.
- **Rato:** Time.
- **Recorrerlo:** Walk it.
- **Recuperara:** Recover.
- **Resbalar:** Slip.
- **Revisé:** Checked.
- **Rodar:** Roll.
- **Rodear:** Go around.
- **Ruta:** Route.
- **Salirme:** Exit.
- **Salto:** Jump.
- **Subir:** Climb.
- **Trasera:** Back.
- **Una vez:** Once.
- **Venas:** Veins.
- **Vendría:** Come.
- **Verlo:** See it.
- **Visión:** Vision.
- **Volando:** Flying.

Questions about the story

1. ¿Qué le gustaba manejar a Daniel?

    a.   Auto.
    b.   Bicicleta.
    c.   Motos.
    d.   Patinetas.

2. ¿A dónde se dirigió Daniel?

    a.   A la montaña.
    b.   A la playa.
    c.   Al bosque.
    d.   Ninguno de los anteriores.

3. ¿Qué le pasó a la bicicleta de Daniel?

    a.   Se dañó.
    b.   Se oxidó.
    c.   Se rayó.
    d.   Ninguno de los anteriores.

4. ¿Qué le pasó a Daniel en el paseo?

    a.   Tuvo un accidente.
    b.   No le paso nada.
    c.   Se encontró a un amigo.
    d.   (sentence doesn´t make sense).

5. ¿Quién rescata a Daniel?

    a.   Un desconocido llamado Eduardo.
    b.   Un desconocido llamado Jose.
    c.   Un desconocido llamado Carlos.
    d.   Nadie.

Answers

1. **B - What did Daniel like to drive?**
2. **A - Where did Daniel go?**
3. **A -What happened to Daniel's bicycle?**
4. **A - What happened to Daniel on the trip?**
5. **D - Who rescues Daniel?**

Chapter Twenty-Five

Basic Vocabulary

Una historia de guerra/A War Story

H ola, hoy les contaré una historia de un **emotivo** viaje a las Islas Malvinas que hice con mi **tío** hace ya unos años. Vamos a empezar, mi nombre es Christopher y esta historia **cuenta** un **viaje** que **ocurrió** cuando tenía **aproximadamente** 10 años hace ya 15 años. **Intentaré recordar** todo con el mayor **detalle** posible, pero **seguramente** hay cosas que quedaron **borradas** para siempre. Todo empezó por una **tarea** que nos **encargaron** en la **escuela primaria** para el acto del 2 de abril. Ese día, en Argentina se **conmemora** la Guerra de Malvinas; para quien no lo **sepa**, fue un **enfrentamiento bélico** que tuvo mi país **contra** el **Reino Unido** en 1982 por la **soberanía** de las Islas Malvinas, o Falkland Islands como le llaman los **británicos**. Al ser una **fecha patria** las escuelas siempre hacen que los **alumnos** hagan un **trabajo temático basado** en lo que pasó en la guerra.

Yo siempre hacía lo **mismo**; **entrevistaba** a mi tío Andrés, ya que había **combatido** en la guerra. **Obviamente,** mis trabajos siempre **recibían** más atención porque tenían el relato de un **ex-soldado.** No era **información** en Internet, era la **voz** de **alguien** que **realmente** estuvo en la guerra, **armado, atrincherado** y **muerto** de **frío.** Aclaro algo importante para **entender** no solo mi historia; sino la de la Guerra de las Malvinas.

Los soldados **argentinos** que fueron desplegados no eran realmente soldados, eran **chicos** de 18 años **seleccionados** al **azar.** Todo chico de esa edad **recibió** un número que luego se **sorteaba** por la televisión y la radio. Si tu número **salía,** tenías que ir sin **preparación,** sin **equipamiento,** sin **defensas,** caminaban **derecho** hacia la **muerte.** En aquella **época** el país estaba bajo una **dictadura militar** que **ideó** una guerra imposible de **ganar,** una guerra **absurda** e **innecesaria.**

Mi tío tuvo mala **suerte** y su número salió sorteado. Volviendo a mi historia; ese año logré que mi tío **acepte venir** a hablar a mi **aula delante** de todos mis **compañeros.** No recuerdo mucho de la **charla** ni que contó específicamente. Todos aplaudimos cuando él terminó, los **profesores** también. Solo **recuerdo** una cosa que dijo en ese momento y es que estaba por ir de viaje a las Malvinas nuevamente.

Por primera **vez** en más de 20 años **desde** la guerra, iba a **volver** a **pisar** esa **isla. Inmediatamente** supe que quería **acompañarlo,** y él aceptó. **Tuvimos** que hacer algunos **esfuerzos** para **convencer** a mis padres, pero finalmente me dejaron ir. Fuimos **solo** nosotros dos. Mi tío **nunca** se **casó** ni tuvo hijos. El viaje fue en auto hasta el Sur.

No recuerdo exactamente **hasta dónde**, mientras **bajábamos** por la costa argentina el frío se hacía cada vez más presente,. Viajamos en un pequeño **avión** para llegar a las islas. Recuerdo que había mucho **viento** y el avión **temblaba** y se **sacudía** como si fuese de **plástico**. Mi tío **bromeó** luego diciendo que ese viaje fue más peligroso que toda la guerra.

Nos quedamos en una pequeña **cabaña**, un hotel no muy **lujoso**, una especie de pequeño **departamento** con dos **camas**. El viaje era solo por dos días. Llegamos el **sábado** por la mañana y el **domingo** a la noche teníamos que **irnos**. Lo primero que hicimos fue ir al **Cementerio** de Darwin, donde están los argentinos **caídos durante** la guerra. Vimos todas las **cruces** blancas. Mi tío **señaló un par** que conocía, me dijo que hubo más **muertos** por **suicidios después** de la guerra que **durante la misma**.

¡Qué estúpidos! **Pensé** en ese momento. No entendí cómo alguien que **sobrevivió** a algo tan horrible como la guerra **pudiese acabar** con su **propia** vida cuando ya estaba a **salvo**. Yo era demasiado pequeño y no entendía mucho **sobre** la vida. El resto del viaje fue aburrido. Hacía mucho frío. No había mucho para hacer. Desde pequeños, nosotros, los argentinos escuchamos Malvinas y es como una **tierra** mágica, **desconocida**, algo que forma parte de nuestro **país**, pero al mismo tiempo no forma parte.

Un lugar que la **mayoría** de los argentinos **recuerda** y **reclama**, pero que nadie conoce realmente. La verdad es que me **decepcionó** un poco,. Yo esperaba algo mágico o **exótico**,

Era un pedazo de tierra **nublada**, fría, **húmeda**. Hicimos un par de cosas más tan poco **relevantes** que ni las recuerdo. En la noche comimos algo en el hotel. Me hice amigo del hijo del **dueño** del lugar. Steven se llamaba. No recuerdo el nombre del padre. Mi inglés de primaria no **sirvió** mucho para la conversación, pero básicamente nos **entendimos** bien y nos **llevábamos** bien. Jugamos videojuegos de fútbol, en el PlayStation 1 que tenía él, la misma que yo tenía en mi casa de Buenos Aires. Jugamos un par de partidos e incluso hicimos un Inglaterra vs Argentina, el cual gané. **Me acuerdo** que **sentí** una **satisfacción**, como si esa **victoria** en el PlayStation fuese un triunfo **importantísimo**, una **especie** de segundo round de la Guerra de las Malvinas. Se sintió igual la victoria de Argentina contra Inglaterra en el **Mundial** '86, con la mano de **Dios** y el gol del **siglo**.

"Maradona, Diego Maradona", **decía** mucho Steven, como si fuese lo único que **conocía** de mi país. Si la historia hubiera **ocurrido** unos años **después** también diría "Messi, Lionel Messi", que en ese momento **recién** estaba empezando su **carrera**. Mi tío no tuvo **problemas** con que vaya a jugar a la casa. Dijo que después volviera a nuestro pequeño departamento que estaba en el mismo **complejo**. El padre de Steven era un hombre tranquilo. Nos miraba jugar sin decir nada.

No recuerdo que haya dicho nada en toda la **noche**. En un momento de **confianza**, le dije a Steven que mi tío era un **héroe**, que había peleado en la guerra. Me respondió que su papá también y que después de la guerra, había **decidido quedarse** allí, en Malvinas. Cuando dijo eso **intenté irme lo antes posible**. Me sentí como un **traidor** en la casa del enemigo; jugando videojuegos y **tomando** Coca-Cola.

Lo sentí como una **traición** a mi tío y como una traición a mi país. Cuando pude **escapé** de ahí y volví con mi tío todo **sobresaltado** y emocionado. Le conté que el dueño del lugar donde nos quedábamos era un enemigo, era un **inglés**. Mi tío no le dió mucha **importancia**, ni siquiera recuerdo si dijo algo. Al igual que el inglés, no era un hombre de muchas **palabras**. Nos fuimos a dormir, **mejor dicho**, él se fué a dormir **incluso roncando**. Yo no pude **dormir**, me sentía **literalmente** en el **campo** enemigo, con ellos durmiendo a **metros de distancia**, como si en **cualquier momento pudiesen entrar** al **cuarto** o tirarnos una **granada**. **Tal vez** todos los **videojuegos** de **disparos** y guerra que jugaba en **esa época** me **afectaron demasiado**, pero estaba **asustado**, con la **adrenalina alta** y mis piernas no se podían quedar **quietas**.

Mi tío **llevaba** siempre una **navaja** con él. La miré en su **mesa**. El resto de la noche me quedé mirándola, un poco más tranquilo al saber que, ante un **hipotético** ataque, **tendríamos** algo para **defendernos**. Con ese **pensamiento**, me quedé dormido. Cuando me **desperté** al día siguiente, mi tío no estaba. Miré alrededor de nuestro pequeño departamento y no había **rastro** de él. **Supuse** que estaba **desayunando** y fuí al pequeño restaurante donde servían el **desayuno**.

Mientras caminaba el complejo, vi a Steven jugando a la pelota solo. Me hizo un **gesto** para que me **uniera**. Me llamó, pero yo todavía **sorprendido** por las **revelaciones** de ayer lo **ignore**. Hice como que no lo veía y seguí caminando. **Efectivamente** mi tío estaba desayunando. **Sorprendentemente**, estaba sentado con el padre de Steven hablando normalmente, como si no se **hubiesen** querido **matar** 20 años atrás. **Me acerqué** y me senté a su lado.

Hablaban en inglés y rápido, no pude entender nada. Cuando se **fué**, intenté saber de qué hablaban, qué **había pasado**, pero mi tío no me **contó nada**. Lo único que me dijo fue que el papá de Steven era un buen hombre. Más tarde recorrimos un poco más las Malvinas y nos preparamos para irnos. Un rato antes de que nos vayamos, Steven **tocó** la **puerta** y me **preguntó tímidamente** si quería jugar al fútbol un **ratito**. Yo **dudé** durante unos **segundos**, pero mi tío me dijo que vaya. Jugamos un rato y al **final** mi tío y el padre de Steven se unieron.

Pateamos unos **penales**. **Años** más **tarde**, vi esa misma **escena** en un videoclip de Paul McCartney, el de Pipes of Peace, donde, durante la Primera Guerra Mundial, se hizo un **cese al fuego** y **ambos bandos** jugaron al fútbol. Paul **interpreta** dos **versiones** de **sí mismo**, una **inglesa** y otra **alemana**. Por la magia de Google me enteré que el videoclip estuvo **inspirado** en una **tregua** que realmente **ocurrió** durante la Primera Guerra Mundial. En la **Navidad** de 1914 **se declaró** un cese al fuego y varios soldados de ambos lados jugaron al fútbol para **festejar**. **Al principio**, mi viaje a Malvinas me pareció una simple **aventura**, la **oportunidad** de conocer las islas que tanto **significaban** para nosotros los argentinos.

Entendí varios años después que para mi tío fue mucho más importante. Fue una manera de **cerrar** ese **capítulo**, de **enfrentarse** a su pasado y de hacer las **paces** con su pasado de **combatiente**. También **aprendí cosas**, aprendí que no hay **bandos** realmente, que no somos enemigos de los ingleses, que no están ellos por un lado, y nosotros por el otro, que todos somos personas y que la guerra es algo que nos **supera**, que no podemos **manejar**. Como dice la canción de Paul McCartney: "Help them see that the people here are just like you and me." La **traducción sería**, "**Ayúdalos** a ver que la **gente** de **acá** es **igual** a ti y a mí". ¿Qué **ironía** no? **Terminé** la historia sobre las Malvinas **citando** un músico **británico**, pero bueno. Eso es todo por hoy. Adiós.

Resumen de la historia

Christopher es un joven que de niño hizo un viaje que le cambió la vida. Cuando era niño, por una tarea escolar entrevistó a su tío que era un ex-combatiente de la guerra de las Malvinas. Su tío tenía planeado ir a las islas y Christopher decide acompañarlo. Conocen la isla y se hacen amigos de Steven y su padre. Christopher y Steven se convierten en amigos, pero todo cambia cuando Steven dice que su padre es un ex-militar inglés que también combatió en la guerra. Christopher quedó aterrado porque pensaba que estaba con el enemigo traicionando su país. Lleno de miedo se va a dormir, pensando que algo malo le pasaría. Por la mañana siguiente despierta buscando a su tío. Para su sorpresa él estaba hablando cordialmente con el padre de Steven, dos antiguos enemigos compartiendo una charla, demostrándoles a los chicos que se puede vivir sin prejuicio ni odio.

Summary of the story

Christopher is a young man who as a child made a trip that changed his life. As a kid, he interviewed his uncle, an Falklands War veteran. His uncle decided to go to the Islands, and Christopher went along with him. They get to know the island and become friends with Steven and his father. Christopher and Steven became friends, but everything changes when Steven says his father is an English veteran as well. Christopher is terrified because he thinks he is with the enemy betraying his country. Full of fear, he goes to sleep thinking that something bad could happen to him. The next morning he wakes up looking for his uncle and to his surprise, he was talking friendly with Steven's father, two former enemies just talking casual, showing the boys that it is possible to live without prejudice and hatred.

Vocabulary List

- **Absurda:** Absurd
- **Acá:** Here.
- **Acabar:** Finish.
- **Acepte:** Accept.
- **Acerqué:** I approached.
- **Acompañarlo:** Accompany him.
- **Adrenalina:** Adrenaline.
- **Afectaron:** Affected.
- **Al:** To.
- **Alemana:** German.
- **Alguien:** Someone.
- **Alta:** Tall/High.
- **Alumnos:** Students.
- **Ambos:** Both.
- **Años:** Years.
- **Aplaudimos:** We applaud.
- **Aprendí:** I learned.
- **Aproximadamente:** Approximately.
- **Argentinos:** Argentineans.
- **Armado:** Armed.
- **Asustado:** Scared.
- **Atrincherado:** Barricaded.
- **Aula:** Classroom.
- **Aventura:** Adventure.
- **Avión:** Airplane.
- **Ayer:** Yesterday.
- **Ayúdalos:** Help them.
- **Azar: By** Chance/Random.
- **Bajábamos:** We were going down.
- **Bandos:** Sides.
- **Basado:** Based.
- **Bélico:** Warlike.
- **Borradas:** Deleted.
- **Británico:** British.
- **Bromeó:** Joked.
- **Cabaña:** Hut / Cabin
- **Caídos:** Fallen.
- **Camas:** Beds.
- **Campo:** Country side
- **Capítulo:** Chapter.
- **Carrera:** Career.
- **Casó:** Married
- **Cementerio:** Cemetery.
- **Cerrar:** Close.
- **Cese Al Fuego:** Cease Fire.
- **Charla:** Talk.
- **Chicos:** Guys.
- **Citando:** Quoting.
- **Combatido:** Fought
- **Combatiente:** Fighter.

- **Compañeros:** Fellows
- **Complejo:** Complex.
- **Confianza:** Trust.
- **Conmemora:** Commemorate.
- **Conocía:** knew.
- **Contó:** Said
- **Contra:** Against.
- **Convencer:** Convince.
- **Cosas:** Things.
- **Cruces:** Crosses.
- **Cualquier:** Any.
- **Cuarto:** Room.
- **Cuenta:** Account.
- **Decepcionó:** Disappointed.
- **Decía:** said.
- **Decidido:** Decided.
- **Declaró:** Declared.
- **Defendernos:** Defend.
- **Defensas:** Defenses.
- **Dejaron:** Left.
- **Delante:** In front.
- **Demasiado:** Too much.
- **Departamento:** Department.
- **Derecho:** Right / straight ahead
- **Desayunando:** Having Breakfast.
- **Desayuno:** Breakfast.
- **Desconocida:** Unknown.
- **Desde:** From.
- **Desperté:** Woke up.
- **Después:** After.
- **Detalle:** Detail / specific
- **Dictadura:** Dictatorship.
- **Dios:** God.
- **Disparos: Gun** Shots.
- **Distancia:** Distance.
- **Domingo:** Sunday.
- **Dónde:** Where.
- **Dormir:** Sleep.
- **Dudé:** Hesitate
- **Dueño:** Owner.
- **Durante:** During

- **Efectivamente:** In fact
- **Emotivo:** Touching.
- **Encargaron:** Ordered.
- **Enfrentamiento:** Confrontation.
- **Enfrentarse:** Confronting.
- **Entender:** Understand.
- **Entendí:** I understood.
- **Entendimos:** We understood.
- **Entrar:** Enter.
- **Entrevistaba:** Interview.
- **Época:** Time/Period/Era.
- **Equipamiento:** Equipment.
- **Esa:** That.
- **Escapé:** I escaped.
- **Escena:** Scene.
- **Escuela:** School.
- **Esfuerzo:** Effort.
- **Especie:** Species / kind
- **Exótico:** Exotic.
- **Ex soldado:** Ex-soldier.
- **Fecha Patria:** Homeland Date.
- **Festejar:** Celebrate.
- **Final:** End.
- **Frío:** Cold.
- **From:** Desde
- **Ganar:** Win.
- **Gente:** People.
- **Gesto:** Gesture.
- **Granada:** Grenade.
- **Había:** There was.
- **Hasta:** To.
- **Héroe:** Hero
- **Hipotético:** Hypothetical.
- **Hubiesen:** Hubiesen.
- **Húmeda:** Wet.
- **Ideó:** Think out.
- **Ignoré:** Ignored.
- **Igual:** Same.
- **Importancia:** Importance.
- **Importantísimo:** Very Important.
- **Incluso:** Even.

- **Información:** Information
- **Inglés:** English.
- **Inmediatamente:** Immediately.
- **Innecesaria:** Unnecessary.
- **Inspirado:** Inspired.
- **Intentaré:** I will try.
- **Intenté:** I tried.
- **Interpreta:** Interpret.
- **Irme: I** Go.
- **Irnos: We** Go
- **Ironía:** Irony.
- **Isla:** Island.
- **La Misma:** The Same.
- **Literalmente:** Literally
- **Llevaba:** / carrying
- **Llevábamos:** We were carrying.
- **Lo Antes Posible:** As Soon As Possible.
- **Lujoso:** Luxury.
- **Manejar:** Drive.
- **Matar:** Kill
- **Mayoría:** Majority.
- **Me Acuerdo:** I Remember.
- **Mejor Dicho:** Best Said.
- **Mesa:** Table.
- **Metros:** meters.
- **Militar:** Military.
- **Mismo:** Same.
- **Momento:** Moment.
- **Muerte:** Death.
- **Muerto:** Dead.
- **Mundial:** World.
- **Nada:** Nothing.
- **Navaja:** blade.
- **Navidad:** Christmas.
- **Noche:** Night.
- **Nublada:** Cloudy.
- **Nunca:** Never.
- **Obviamente:** Obviously.
- **Ocurrido:** Occurred.
- **Ocurrió:** Occurred.
- **Oportunidad:** Opportunity.
- **Paces:** Peace.
- **País:** Country.
- **Palabras:** Words.
- **Par:** Pair.
- **Pasado:** Past.
- **Pateamos:** We kicked.
- **Penales:** Penalties.
- **Pensamiento:** Thought.
- **Pensé: I** Thought
- **Pisar:** Stepping on.
- **Plástico:** Plastic.
- **Preguntó:** Asked.
- **Preparación:** Preparation / training
- **Primaria:** Primary school.
- **Principio:** Beginning.
- **Problemas:** Problems.
- **Profesores:** Teachers.
- **Propia:** Own.
- **Pudiese:** could
- **Pudiesen:** Could
- **Puerta:** Door.
- **Quedarse:** Stay
- **Quietas:** Still
- **Rastro:** Trail.
- **Ratito:** A short time
- **Realmente:** Actually.
- **Recibían:** Received.
- **Recibió:** Received.
- **Recién:** A moment ago
- **Reclama:** Claim.
- **Recordar:** Recall.
- **Recorrimos:** We visited.
- **Recuerda:** Remember.
- **Recuerdo:** Remember.
- **Reino:** Kingdom
- **Relevantes:** Relevant.
- **Revelaciones:** Revelations.
- **Roncando:** Snoring.
- **Sábado:** Saturday.
- **Sacudía:** Shaking.

- **Salía:** Exit.
- **Salvó:** Saved.
- **Satisfacción:** Satisfaction.
- **Segundos:** Seconds.
- **Seguramente:** Surely.
- **Seleccionados:** Selected.
- **Sentí:** Felt.
- **Señaló:** Signed.
- **Sepa:** Know.
- **Seria:** Seria.
- **Sí Mismo:** Self.
- **Siglo:** Century.
- **Significaban:** Meant.
- **Sirvió:** Served.
- **Soberanía:** Sovereignty.
- **Sobre:** About.
- **Sobresaltado:** Outstanding.
- **Sobrevivió:** Survived.
- **Sólo:** Alone.
- **Sorprendentemente:** Surprisingly.
- **Sorprendido:** Surprised.
- **Sorteaba:** Surprised.
- **Suerte:** Luck.
- **Suicidios:** Suicides.
- **Supera:** Overcomes.
- **Supuse:** Supposed.
- **Tal Vez:** Maybe.
- **Tarde:** Late
- **Tarea:** Homework
- **Temático:** Thematic.
- **Temblaba:** Trembled.
- **Tendríamos:** We would have.
- **Termine:** Finish.
- **Tierra:** Earth.
- **Tímidamente:** Shyly.
- **Tío:** Uncle.
- **Tirarnos:** Throw us.
- **Tocó:** Touched.
- **Tomando:** Taking.
- **Trabajo:** Work.
- **Traducción:** Translation.
- **Traición:** Betrayal.
- **Traidor:** Traitor.
- **Tregua:** Truce.
- **Tuvimos:** We had.
- **Unido:** United.
- **Uniera:** bond
- **Venir:** Come
- **Versiones:** Versions
- **Vez:** Time.
- **Viaje:** Travel/Trip.
- **Victoria:** Victory.
- **Videojuegos:** Video Games.
- **Viento:** Wind.
- **Volver:** Back
- **Voz:** Voice

Questions about the story

1. ¿Cuál es la nacionalidad de Christopher?

    a. Mexicano.
    b. Ingles.
    c. Argentino.
    d. Chileno.

2. ¿Qué era su tío?

    a. Un mecánico.
    b. Un profesor.
    c. Un ex-soldado.
    d. Ninguno de los anteriores.

3. ¿A dónde viajaron?

    a. Buenos Aires.
    b. Londres.
    c. Manchester.
    d. Ninguno de los anteriores.

4. ¿Qué países participaron en la guerra de las Malvinas?

    a. Estados Unidos vs Argentina.
    b. Estados Unidos vs Inglaterra.
    c. Argentina vs Inglaterra.
    d. Inglaterra vs Alemania.

5. ¿Cómo se llama el amigo de Christopher en la historia?

    a. Steve.
    b. Stve.
    c. Steven.
    d. Steeve.

Answers

1. **C - What is Christopher's nationality?**
2. **C - What was his Uncle?**
3. **D - Where did they travel to?**
4. **C - Which countries participated in the Falklands War?**
5. **C - What is the name of Christopher's friend in the story?**

140

Conclusion

Well, there you have it my friend! 25 Spanish Short Stories that have no doubt built your vocabulary in a real world, practical sense.
I hope you're excited to start using your new found vocabulary with some natives - and remember, its completely fine to make mistakes!

The way that this book is set up may seem unusual to anyone who has studied Spanish using traditional methods (ala Death By Grammar), but just take a good look at how long traditional Spanish learners take to make any real progress, let alone reach fluency.

Do you really want to move forward at a snail's pace? I think not!

Be sure to revisit the stories often so you can internalize the lessons and vocabulary. We even recommend that write some of your own!

You now have the most effective Spanish learning tool in the world at your fingertips. New Spanish language learners that become fluent in 3 months follow these methods and use this kind of material – not the traditional ones.
Make sure you do to.

By internalizing the lessons in these stories there is no reason why you won't be speaking conversational Spanish in a few months - instead of years like other students!

I wish you good luck on your Spanish journey. Hasta luego!

<u>Did you enjoy the book?</u>

We want to thank you for purchasing and reading this book, we really hope you got a lot out of it.

If you did, would you mind leaving a quick one-sentence review on Amazon for us?

It'll take you less than 1 minute and it really does make a HUGE difference.

As a small start-up publishing company with a tiny budget we rely solely on readers, like you, to leave feedback on our book.

We read all of our reviews, so we would love to hear from you!

Just scan the QR code with your phone camera below and get teleported our Amazon review page instantly:

Thanks so much,
Fluency Faster

Made in the USA
Middletown, DE
08 March 2022

62339024R00090